The Arms
of the
Scottish Bishoprics
by
Rev. W. T. Lyon M.A., F.S.A. (Scot)
with a foreword by
The Most Revd. W. J. F. Robberds D.D.,
Bishop of Brechin, and Primus of the Episcopal
Church of Scotland.

First Published in 1917
A facsimile copy produced and privately printed by
The Armorial Register Limited 2017

First Published in 2017
by
The Armorial Register Limited
All rights reserved

Text & Images Copyright The Armorial Register Limited

No part of this work may be photocopied, stored in a retrieval system, published, performed in public, adapted, broadcast, transmitted, recorded or reproduced in any form or by any means, without the permission of the copyright owner.

The rights of The Armorial Register Limited to be identified as author and illustrator of this work has been asserted in accordance with the Copy-right, Design and Patents Act 1988

ISBN: 978-0-9957246-2-4

British Library Cataloguing-in-Publication Data
A catalogue record of this book is available on request from the British Library

THE ARMS OF THE SCOTTISH BISHOPRICS.

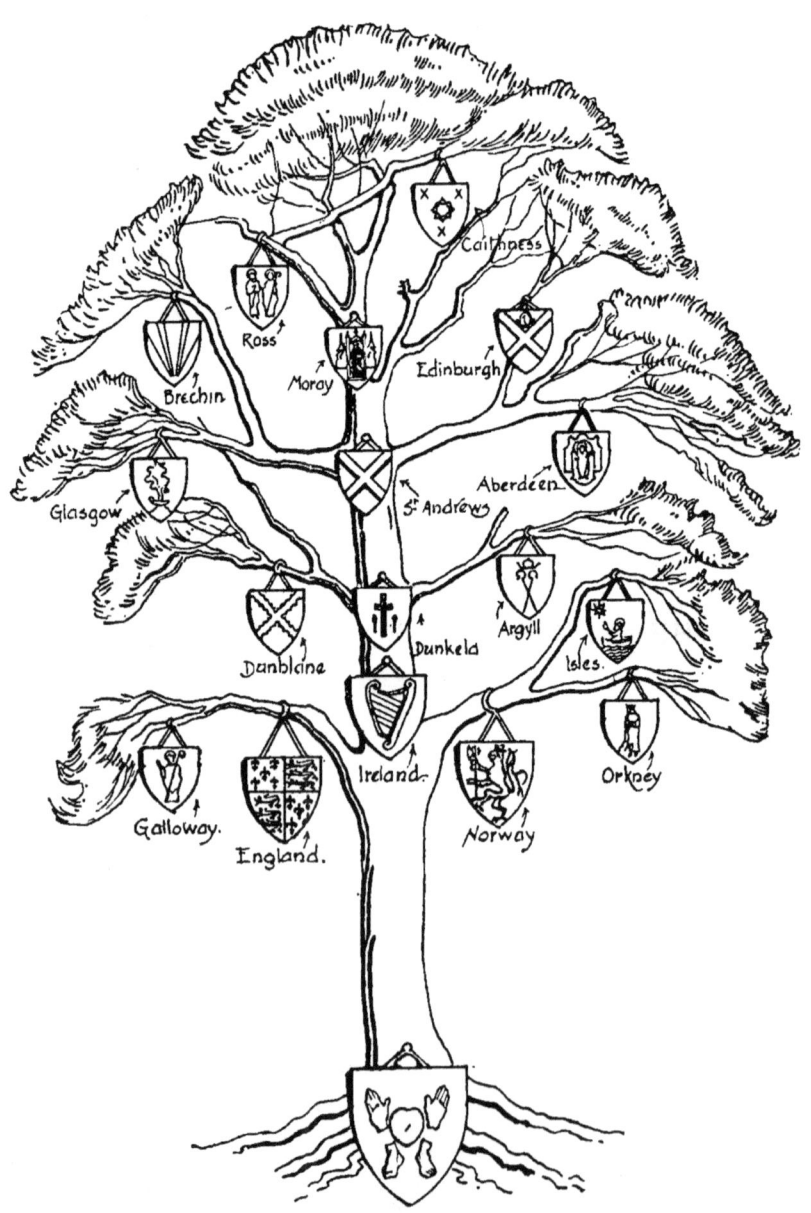

THE ARMS

OF THE

SCOTTISH BISHOPRICS

BY

Rev. W. T. LYON, M.A., F.S.A. (Scot.)

WITH A FOREWORD BY

The Most Revd. W. J. F. ROBBERDS, D.D.,
Bishop of Brechin, and Primus of the Episcopal
Church in Scotland.

ILLUSTRATED BY

A. C. CROLL MURRAY.

SELKIRK:
"THE SCOTTISH CHRONICLE" OFFICES.

1917.

To

I. R. L.

PREFACE.

THE following chapters appeared in the pages of " The Scottish Chronicle " in 1915 and 1916, and it is owing to the courtesy of the Proprietor and Editor that they are now republished in book form.

Their original publication in the pages of a Church newspaper will explain something of the lines on which the book is fashioned. The articles were written to explain and to describe the origin and development of the Armorial Bearings of the ancient Dioceses of Scotland. These Coats of arms are, and have been more or less continuously, used by the Scottish Episcopal Church since they came into use in the middle of the 17th century, though whether the disestablished Church has a right to their use or not is a vexed question. Fox-Davies holds that the Church of Ireland and the Episcopal Church in Scotland lost their diocesan Coats of Arms on disestablishment, and that the Welsh Church will suffer the same loss when the Disestablishment Act comes into operation (Public Arms). Stevenson, on the other hand, says with regard to the Scottish Diocesan Arms that it has never been actually decided who, if anybody, has the right to use them (Heraldry in Scotland). It was therefore considered best to take for granted the customary use of the Arms—whether right or wrong—by the Episcopal Church, and to explain and describe their development. In view of the uncertainty, however, it was thought best to trace the course of their development only down to the Disestablishment, so readers will understand that when the Seals of post-Reformation Bishops are referred to, the reference is confined to those Prelates who ruled between the Reformation and the Revolution. A chapter was added in which the legal question of ownership is discussed.

It is hoped that the book as a whole will be of interest to Scottish Ecclesiologists, though the last two chapters bear more particularly on the Episcopal Church and its customary use of the Arms.

Of the scope of the book, it is not necessary to say more than a few words. It is not intended to be a manual of Heraldry, or even of Ecclesiastical Heraldry, but only an account of a rather neglected bypath of Scottish Ecclesiology—even Woodward in his " Ecclesiastical Heraldry " devotes only a few pages to Scotland. Again, it is not to be regarded as a Church History : as a rule the history of a diocese is referred to only when it has some bearing on its coat of Arms, or on the seals of its Bishop or Chapter.

The Heraldic " Tree " which appears as the frontispiece is, of course, an anachronism : with the exception of Edinburgh, no Scottish Diocese possessed a Coat of Arms for centuries after its foundation. The Tree, however, illustrates the growth of the Scottish Bishoprics : at the root of the Tree are the traditional Arms of Christ, from whom all originate; the three immediate sources, Ireland, England, and Norway are shown by the Arms of those countries on the trunk and lowest branches of the Tree. From the Irish foundation at Iona the Primacy of the Scottish Church was transferred to Dunkeld, where Tuathal, " Primus Episcopus," ruled in the 9th century; from Dunkeld the Primacy passed to the " Bishops of the Scots " at St. Andrews, from whose diocese the majority of the Scottish sees were taken. The Diocese of Galloway was subject to the English Archbishop of York, and the Dioceses of Orkney and the Isles to the Norwegian Archbishop of Trondhjem until the later middle ages. The fourteen bishoprics indicated by their shields make up the branches of the one tree of Ecclesia Scoticana, typified by the Scots Fir Tree.

Of the many books consulted, special acknowledgment must be made to Laing's "Catalogues of Scottish Seals," Macdonald's "Scottish Armorial Seals," "The Arms of the Royal and Parliamentary Burghs of Scotland," by the late Lord Bute, and the historical works of the late Bishop Dowden of Edinburgh.

I have to acknowledge the great kindness of the Primus of the Episcopal Church in Scotland, who in the midst of his multifarious duties has written a foreword to this volume.

During the previous publication of the following chapters, one or two correspondents made suggestions which I have made use of, and for which I would express my thanks.

And lastly, I must tender my warmest gratitude to Mr A. C. Croll Murray of Lanark, who is responsible for the illustrations. Many of the Coats of Arms of the Scottish Bishoprics allow real scope to an artist, and in giving worthy expression to the blazons, Mr Murray has spared no pains and grudged no time, with results which combine exactness of detail with real artistic feeling.

NORTH BERWICK, SEPTEMBER, 1917.

CONTENTS.

	Foreword	... Page	xi.
Chapter 1.	Heraldry	... Page	1
2.	The Language of Heraldry		5
3.	Scottish Church Heraldry		11
4.	St. Andrews		15
5.	Dunkeld		23
6.	Dunblane		27
7.	Edinburgh		31
8.	Aberdeen		33
9.	Orkney		37
10.	Moray		41
11.	Ross		45
12.	Caithness		49
13.	Brechin		53
14.	Glasgow		57
15.	Galloway		67
16.	Argyll		71
17.	The Isles		75
18.	Marshalling		79
19.	The Legal Question		85

ERRATUM.

Page 28—For Laurencekirk in Forfarshire, read Laurencekirk in Kincardineshire.

FOREWORD.

It gives me much pleasure to write a brief introductory word to this book. The science of Heraldry, as Mr Lyon points out, is not as well known in these days as it used to be formerly, and as indeed it deserves to be. But for those who are interested in Scottish ecclesiastical history there is a store of most interesting information contained in the descriptions given by the author, of the Arms which in the course of time came to be adopted by, or attached to, our various Scottish Bishoprics. Such information once again shows that our Church was no importation from England, but that its romantic story is essentially and intimately bound up with the life and history of Scotland. A most useful and valuable chapter is that on " The Language of Heraldry "—for most of us, I expect, an unintelligible and unknown tongue. Under Mr Lyon's guidance we can enter more intelligently into the meanings of the different emblems and their inter-relation, and I think that not a few who read the book will wish that this chapter had been longer and fuller. Another chapter which is likely to attract special attention is that which discusses the legal right of the Episcopal Church to bear Arms, and which contains the author's interesting argument by which he would answer the question he raises in the affirmative. Mr Lyon has given us a book which will, I hope, be widely read and studied, and he deserves the thanks of our fellow Churchpeople for his industry in placing such information, in a compact and attractive form, within their reach.

WALTER J. F. ROBBERDS,
Bishop of Brechin, Primus of the
Episcopal Church in Scotland.

SEPTEMBER, 1917.

CHAPTER I.

Heraldry.

In the middle ages heraldry formed no small part of the education of a gentleman : in fact it was considered indispensible in the upbringing of a knight. In the twentieth century the science is generally neglected, if not scornfully regarded as unpractical in these unromantic times, and nothing more than the conceit of a past age. From the close of the middle ages the history of heraldry, or more properly armory, is one of gradual neglect : and this decay was one of the many incidental results of the discovery of gunpowder, and the consequent revolution of warfare, which led to the abandonment of the practice of wearing armour. During the seventeenth century the growing neglect brought the science into disrepute, until during the eighteenth century, as it has been said, heraldry was abandoned to coach-builders and undertakers.

In modern times there are signs that there is some revival of interest in the subject, but in Scotland particularly, ecclesiastical heraldry is still in a neglected state, due of course to the fact that the ancient dioceses of the national Church have been legally abolished, and the Established Church therefore has no use for the armorial bearings of the discarded sees.

In the Scottish Church there are fourteen dioceses (now governed by seven Bishops), each one of which has a shield of arms, and each of these escutcheons has a history and a meaning, many of them of great interest. Yet their significance is comparatively unknown. Why does the Diocese of St. Andrews bear a *white* saltire on a *blue* ground? Who are the two figures on the shield of the Diocese of Ross intended to represent?

Before we enter on the discussion of the significance of the armorial bearings of the various dioceses, it will be necessary to clear some preliminary ground as to the origin of heraldry in general, and especially to explain the technical terms used in the science.

Tradition ascribes the origin of heraldry to a very early period of history. The mediæval heralds assigned arms to many of the classical heroes, as Julius Cæsar, Alexander, and Hector, Prince of Troy; to David, King of Israel; Joshua; the three wise men or Kings who came to welcome the new-born Christ; to the Apostles, and many other prominent men of the Bible from Adam onwards. In fact they did not scruple to assign arms to the Son of God himself, viz., The wounded Heart, between pierced Hands and Feet arranged saltirewise. These arms are worthy of notice, not only as a heraldic curiosity, but also because they are sometimes to be seen in ancient buildings. They are also interesting because they reflect the feeling of the middle ages that every man who could lay claim to gentle birth must necessarily have a right to bear arms; and Christ could lay claim to descent from the ancient royal family of Judah. In the " Boke of St. Alban's " (1488) we read, " Of the offspringe of the gentilman Japeth came Habraham, Moyses, Aron, and the profettys, and also the Kyng of the right lyne of Mary, of whom that Gentilman Jhesus was borne very God and man : after his manhode Kyng of the londe of Jude and of Jues, gentilman by his Modre Mary, Prynce of cote-armure."

Without doubt the germ or idea of heraldry is of very ancient origin. There are indications of it in the ensigns of the twelve tribes of Israel: in the directions for the pitching of the camp in the wilderness as recorded in the second chapter of Numbers, it was laid down that " Every man of the children of Israel shall pitch by his own standard, with the ensign of their father's house."* We find it again in the Eagles of the Roman army, and in the distinguishing devices of the legions. In our own country the tartans and badges of the clans bear witness to the almost universal desire of men to bear some distinguishing mark or badge to denote the gens to which they belong; and it was in this desire that heraldry as we know it took its origin.

The real beginnings of heraldry as a scientific system cannot be traced farther back than the twelfth century. It was intimately connected with chivalry, and it came into being to meet the needs of the knights who took part in the tournaments, and who fought in the wars of the Crusades.

When taking part in the tournament, the knight was completely hidden within his armour, and the convenience of a distinguishing badge soon became obvious. Again, in the first two crusades, when knights of many nations were engaged in the same adventure, the need for some distinctive badge must have become imperative, so that we find in the third crusade (1189) some sort of armorial bearings depicted on the shields of many of the knights. From the end of the twelfth century the custom of bearing arms became general, and was early adopted by Ecclesiastics, and indeed by all men of noble birth, so that

---

* It has been suggested that the phrase "*Lion of the Tribe of Judah*" has a reference to the ensign of that tribe. The identification of Christ as the King with the tribal emblem finds parallels in later times, *e.g.*, in Aytoun's "Lays of the Scottish Cavaliers," "*Edinburgh after Flodden*":—

No Scottish foot went backward
When the royal Lion fell.

the right to wear " Coat-armour " came to be recognised as a sign of gentle birth, and armorial bearings became hereditary in families, and were handed down from father to son. Armorial bearings were also assumed by city corporations, livery companies, colleges and dioceses; but it must always be borne in mind that *originally* armorial bearings were adopted as a distinctive badge which the knight wore when he went into battle.

CHAPTER II.

The Language of Heraldry.

Heraldry may be said to have a language of its own, but for our purpose it will not be necessary to do more than indicate such terms as will make the study of Scottish diocesan heraldry intelligible.

The " Achievement " is composed of several parts, the Shield, the Helmet, the Mantling, the Crest, and the Supporters.

(1) THE SHIELD. This is the most important item in the heraldic achievement, because it bears the distinctive charges which form the armorial bearings of a family or society. The shape of the shield has varied considerably from the simple " Heater " shape, which was used when the science of heraldry was at its zenith in the middle ages, to the rococo forms of the 18th century, which bore practically no resemblance to a shield at all.

It should be borne in mind that when reference is made to the Dexter (right) and Sinister (left) sides of the shield, the point of view is supposed to be that of the knight holding the shield, i.e., looking over it; so that when we look *towards* a shield of arms, the side which appears to us as the left, is, heraldically speaking, the dexter or right side.

It will be most convenient to deal here, under the heading of " The Shield," with the " Tinctures," " Ordinaries," and " Charges."

(a) THE TINCTURES are metals or colours. As a general rule every shield bears at least both a colour and a metal, the one for the ground, the other for the charge or charges. Metal must not be placed on metal, nor colour on colour[*] : the arms of Jerusalem are the outstanding exception to this rule—the gold crosses on the silver ground—and in all probability they were deliberately adopted as being of a unique character, and therefore appropriate for a kingdom which was unlike all others.

The tinctures with their heraldic names are :—

Metals

    Gold .... Or.
    Silver .... Argent.

Colours

    Red .... Gules.
    Blue .... Azure.
    Black .... Sable.
    Green .... Vert.
    Purple .... Purpure.

Blood colour (Sanguine) and Orange (Tenny) and various Furs are also found in heraldry, but no examples of their use occur in Scottish Diocesan armorial bearings. The expression "Proper" applied to a charge, indicates that it bears its natural colouring; it is often used, for instance, in reference to human figures.

It is interesting to note that the most commonly used tinctures in Scottish as well as in English diocesan heraldry, are argent and azure; and this

[*] Sometimes the charge may be blazoned both of a metal and of a colour : in that case the predominant tincture of the charge must conform to the rule : but minor parts of the charge may form exceptions. For instance, part of the gold crozier held by St. Ninian in the Arms of Galloway is placed directly upon the field which is argent : the figure of the Saint is coloured in accordance with the rule that colour must be placed on metal.

preference is explained—at any rate in the case of Scotland—by the fact that these are the traditional colours both of the Virgin Mary and St. Andrew.

(b) THE ORDINARIES are the simplest kind of heraldic device, being simple geometric figures placed on the shield. Some are called " Honourable " and some " Subordinate " ordinaries, but the distinction between the two classes is not clearly marked, and writers differ as to the group in which certain ordinaries should be included. The following are, however, usually included among the honourable ordinaries :—

(A) THE CHIEF.   (B) THE PALE.   (C) THE FESS.   (D) THE BEND.

(E) THE CHEVRON.   (F) THE SALTIRE.   (G) THE CROSS.

A few of the subordinate ordinaries will also be met with :—

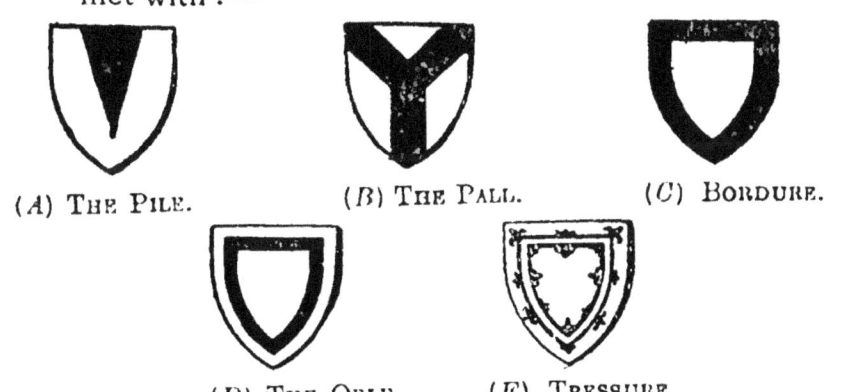

(A) THE PILE.   (B) THE PALL.   (C) BORDURE.

(D) THE ORLE.   (E) TRESSURE.

Most of these ordinaries explain themselves, but the Tressure demands a word of explanation. This device is almost entirely confined to Scottish Heraldry, and is generally known as the Royal Tressure. It is borne on the royal arms of Scotland, and when it appears on the escutcheon of a subject, it is invariably the sign of special royal favour, and often of royal ancestry. It is usually blazoned, "A *double Tressure, flory counter flory,*" indicating that the heads of the fleur-de-lys, which lie behind the tressure, should be drawn alternately pointing towards the middle and the outside of the shield; and they should not appear between the double tressure. The use of the tressure will again be referred to when we reach the heraldry of the Diocese of St. Andrews.

The names of the ordinaries are also used to describe the manner in which a shield is divided: for instance, a shield may be parted *per pale*, i.e., perpendicularly in the centre, as in the diocesan arms of Glasgow and Galloway, or *per chevron* i.e., according to the shape of a chevron. The term *per cross* is not used, *quarterly* being employed instead, as in the case of the Diocese of St. Andrews, Dunkeld, and Dunblane.

The names of the ordinaries are also used with reference to the arrangement of charges on the shield, e.g., the two crosiers arranged *saltirewise* in the arms of Argyll.

(c) CHARGES may be of practically any nature :—
    (1) Living creatures, as men, animals, birds.
    (2) Inanimate charges of all kinds.
    (3) The ordinaries.

Examples of (1) are common in ecclesiastical heraldry, particularly in Scotland, though they are also found in England, as in the case of Our Lord seated upon a throne, depicted on the arms of Chichester, and of St. Mary on the arms of Salisbury. In Scotland effigies of Saints are blazoned on the armorial bearings of no less than six dioceses, Aberdeen, Orkney, Moray, Ross, Galloway, and the Isles.

Of (2) we find examples in the Tree and Bell of Glasgow, the Crown of Thorns of Caithness, the Crosiers of Argyll, and the Passion Nails of Dunkeld.

The saltire of St. Andrews and Edinburgh, the piles of Brechin, and the saltire engrailed of Dunblane are instances of the use of ordinaries.

(2) THE HELMET, which was placed above the shield, need not detain us, as it has no place in ecclesiastical heraldry.* Its place was taken by the " Mitre," which was used, of course, by Bishops and Abbats, or the " Hat," which is usually supposed to be the distinctive mark of a Cardinal. This is a common mistake, as in ecclesiastical heraldry—particularly in foreign countries—the hat is a common feature: the different grades of clergy were distinguished by the colour of the hat, and by the number of tassels hanging from it. The well-known Cardinal's hat is red in colour, and has 15 tassels depending from it on either side.

The use of the ecclesiastical hat in heraldry never became general in Scotland, though there are examples of its use: for instance, Thomas Nidrie, Archdeacon of Moray (1520) bore on his seal above a shield charged with his paternal arms, an ecclesiastical hat adorned with tassels.

(3) THE MANTLING or LAMBREQUIN covered the helmet in order to afford protection from the heat of the sun.

*There are a few exceptions to this rule: both Archbishop Sharp of St. Andrews, and Bishop Leighton of Dunblane used a helmet in their armorial insignia: but the laws of heraldry were not very scrupulously observed in the 17th century.

(4) The Crest as a rule was made of moulded leather, and was worn above the helmet on a wreath or torse.

The mantling and crest, being practically part of the helmet, do not find a place in ecclesiastical heraldry.

(5) Supporters were never used with official diocesan arms, and though it was not an uncommon custom to depict the arms of ecclesiastics as supported by two angels, and though some of the mediæval Bishops and Abbats had, as individuals, the right to supporters, this part of the heraldic achievement falls outside the scope of these pages, which deal with the development of the official arms of the dioceses of the Scottish Church.

The heraldic achievement of a diocese, then, consists of a shield of arms over which is placed a mitre. (N.B.—In the diagrams of the arms of the various dioceses in the following articles, the mitres are copied from those placed above the armorial shields of the Scottish Bishops on the heraldic ceiling of St. Machar's Cathedral at Aberdeen, which dates from 1520.)

CHAPTER III.

Scottish Church Heraldry.

In England it was customary in the middle ages for the dioceses and great abbeys to bear official arms, but in Scotland the practice was adopted only after the reformation. During the mediæval period a Scottish Bishop or Abbat bore a shield charged with his paternal arms, above which he placed a mitre indicative of his office : often, too, a crosier was placed palewise behind the shield, or in some instances two crosiers saltirewise : occasionally this badge of office was incorrectly borne *upon* the shield as an additional charge, as was done by Abbat Hunter of Melrose, whose arms, bearing two crosiers superimposed saltirewise, are still to be seen sculptured on the wall of the South Transept of the Abbey.

There are, however, traces of the occasional use of official arms by the Scottish Ecclesiastics even before the reformation. Many of the Scottish Bishops—particularly in the Highlands—took their titles from the county or province over which they bore spiritual jurisdiction, rather than from their cathedral city, as was the usual Catholic custom. This peculiarity may have originated in the status of a Bishop in the Celtic Church, which was inferior to that of the Abbat of the monastery in which the Bishop lived : the consequence of this arrangement was that the Bishop, though he performed episcopal functions, was not master in his own house (sedes, i.e., see). In course of time the authority of the Bishop increased in the *diocese*, while that of the Abbat became confined to his own *monastery*, and the Bishop came to be identified rather with his *diocese* than with his *see*, and eventually it was the diocese or district which gave him his title.

In some cases the Bishops not only derived their titles from the districts in which they ruled, but they assumed also the armorial bearings of the Lords of the districts as quasi-official diocesan arms, and bore them on their episcopal seals. We shall find instances of this practice in the case of Moray, Ross, and Caithness. In no case, however, did these armorial bearings come to be recognized as official diocesan arms; they were merely used by some—very few—of the Bishops of the respective dioceses to indicate the extent of their jurisdiction. It should be noted, however, that the arms borne by the Diocese of Brechin are identical with those of the ancient Lordship of that name.

But although it must be admitted that the assumption of diocesan arms dates only from the reformation, we can trace the germ of the armorial bearings of almost every diocese. In the majority of cases they are derived from the seals of the mediæval Bishops, and their development can be traced through three stages :—

(1) The earliest episcopal seals which have come down to us bear the figure of a Bishop in the act of benediction.

(2) As time went on, some device allusive to the patron of the cathedral or diocese—usually an effigy of the patron himself—was used as a device on their seals by Bishop after Bishop.

(3) After the reformation these devices were adopted as armorial bearings by the various dioceses. Eight —possibly nine—of the diocesan shields of arms (including that of Edinburgh, as derived from St. Andrews) were evolved in this way.

The adoption of official diocesan arms was probably due to the closer intercourse between England and Scotland which resulted from the union of the Crowns of the two countries in 1603. The practice had been general in England previous to the reformation, and its advantages were no doubt soon recognised by the Scottish Church.

As regards the date of the assumption of arms by the various dioceses, it is not possible to give the exact year in any case. We find during the seventeenth century variations of the arms borne by the Dioceses of Edinburgh, Glasgow, Brechin, and the Isles, which show that they came into use gradually, and, it may be added, without authority. But although we cannot arrive at the exact date of the adoption of the arms of any diocese, there were three distinct stages in the growth of Scottish diocesan heraldry as a whole, and these may be noted in different records of armorial bearings :—

(1) The Register of the Lyon King of Arms. In Scotland the Lord Lyon has, under the crown, the supreme judicial power of regulating the bearing of armorial insignia, and in the year 1672 an act of the Scottish Parliament was passed, ordaining all the nobility and gentry of Scotland to register their armorial bearings in the books of the Lord Lyon under pain of various penalties. In accordance with this act, the arms of the following dioceses, some of which had been assumed many years before, were recorded by the Bishops and are still contained in the Register : St. Andrews, Edinburgh, Ross, Galloway, and Argyll. (N.B.—The legal right of a disestablished Church to bear arms will be discussed in a later chapter.)

(2) The "System of Heraldry," by Nisbet of Dean, published in 1704. This book contains, in addition

to those recorded in the Lyon Register, the arms of Glasgow and Dunblane.

(3) Edmondson's " Body of Heraldry," published in 1780, contains the armorial bearings of the 14 Scottish dioceses, as borne at the present time.

Thus, while some of the dioceses can claim for their armorial bearings an antiquity of almost three centuries, there is no diocese whose arms have not been in use for nearly 150 years.

CHAPTER IV.

St. Andrews.

Tradition connects the town of St. Andrews with the introduction of Christianity into Scotland in the fourth century. The legends of the coming of St. Regulus to this country with the relics of St. Andrew are rather involved, but may be set down as follows :—St. Andrew the Apostle, after many missionary journeys in Scythia, Cappadocia, and Bithynia, came to Patras in Achaia, where among his converts was the wife of the Pro-Consul. Her husband, enraged at her conversion, ordered the Apostle to be crucified on the diagonal cross or saltire, which has since been connected with his name. He was bound with cords to the cross, and lingered for two days, during which he exhorted his converts to remain stedfast in the faith. About 300 years later, according to the Aberdeen Breviary, Regulus was the custodier of the Apostle's relics at Patras : and on the invasion of Patras by Constantine, he was bidden by an angel to hide certain parts of the sacred relics. After Constantine had removed the rest of the relics to Constantinople, the angel again appeared to St. Regulus and bade him take the part of the relics which he had concealed to the "Western Region of the world," where he should found a church in honour of the Apostle on the land where he should suffer shipwreck. We now follow the legend as it is contained in the MS. of the Priory of St. Andrews : After voyaging for a year and a half among the Greek

Islands, on many of which he built oratories to St. Andrew, he at length was wrecked on the shore of the country of the Picts. . . . . Meanwhile, Ungus, son of Unguist, a King of the Picts, was waging war in the Merse (with Athelstane, a Saxon King, according to one tradition). And as the Pictish King was walking with seven companions, the blazing white saltire of St. Andrew appeared in the blue sky, and a voice was heard saying, "Ungus, Ungus, hear me, an Apostle of Christ, called Andrew, who am sent to defend and guard thee." He was also warned in a dream that the relics of St. Andrew would be brought to his kingdom, and that the place where they should rest was to become renowned and honoured. The Picts, being victorious, swore to venerate St. Andrew for ever.

King Ungus gave to St. Regulus or Rule a large part of Kilrymont for the building of churches to God and St. Andrew, the town which in later times was called St. Andrews. The Apostle thus came to be venerated as the Patron Saint of Scotland; and the cross on which he suffered martyrdom, the saltire argent on an azure ground, became the national arms, and in later times the arms of the diocese of St. Andrews, the tinctures of the shield being derived from the mythical appearance to Ungus of the white saltire in the blue sky.

As far as the heraldry of the diocese is concerned, we may make a start with the re-organization of the Church which took place in the reign of Malcolm Ceanmore and his Queen, St. Margaret, and continued during the following reigns. The purpose of this reformation was, of course, to bring the Scottish Church into line with the rest of the Church in the West, with its headquarters at Rome. Turgot, Prior of Durham, who had probably been the Confessor and Biographer of St. Margaret, was consecrated Bishop of St. Andrews in 1109. Although there was as yet no Primacy of St. Andrews, the old title of

" Bishop of the Scots " was retained and appears on the seals of the Bishops as late as 1292 when it was used on the seal of Bishop William Fraser, and this title seems to imply a claim to some sort of metropolitan jurisdiction. Another seal of the same Bishop has the title of " St. Andrews," and this became for the future the general custom. But owing partly to old associations, and partly to the prominent share taken by many Bishops of the diocese in political and international affairs, St. Andrews was throughout the middle ages the most important see in Scotland, even before it was erected into an Archbishopric by Pope Sixtus 4th in 1472.

Bearing in mind, then, the prominent part played by the Bishops of St. Andrews in national affairs, we shall expect to find that many of them have left records in the way of seals. And indeed seals of every mediæval Bishop, with the exception of the first two, Turgot and Robert, have been preserved, some of them of great heraldic interest. The prevailing device is, as might be expected, the Patron Saint of the see : in fact, after the first seven Bishops, every Bishop who ruled the see before the Reformation bore on his seal, or on one of his seals, the device of St. Andrew and his saltire.

The majority of these seals present no particular heraldic interest, though most of them are valuable in that they show the paternal arms of the owner, but four are of great interest to us, as they exhibit armorial bearings possibly assumed for official purposes.

(1) The seal of William de Landallis, who was consecrated in 1342.

(1371.) St. Andrew crucified, between two shields each bearing the royal arms, the sinister shield being differenced with a staff and sceptre or two crosiers in saltire over all. This shield, according to Birch (History of Scottish Seals), must be accepted as the first shield of arms of the see. Probably, however, Birch was in error when he regarded the shield mentioned above as the official arms of the see, because as far as we know such a shield occurs nowhere else; but we may regard it as a shield assumed by the Bishop to denote his office as Bishop of the leading diocese of the kingdom of Scotland.

In the base of the vesica-shaped seal is a Bishop kneeling in prayer between two shields, both of them charged with the Bishop's paternal arms, viz., an Orle. And the interest is this, on the dexter shield within the Orle is a saltire. The question then arises, was this saltire assumed in allusion to his occupying the see of St. Andrews, and had the cross of St. Andrew come to be recognised as the badge of the diocese?

(2) Bishop John Kennedy, translated from Dunkeld to St. Andrews in 1440, has left two seals. In the base of the one there is the figure of a Bishop between two shields bearing the paternal arms of Kennedy, viz., a chevron between three cross crosslets fitchée. On the dexter shield, the paternal arms are placed within the royal tressure. On the other seal is a shield of the Bishop's paternal arms within the royal tressure, surmounted by a mitre.

(3) Bishop Patrick Graham, translated from Brechin to St. Andrews in 1465, who became first Archbishop in 1472, continued the practice of Bishop Kennedy, and bore on his seal his paternal arms, viz., on a chief engrailed, three escallop shells, within the royal tressure.

Now this suggests an interesting question, Was it by virtue of their tenure of the see, which had originally been known as the Bishopric of the Scots, that they bore the honourable augmentation of the tressure of the *King* of Scots, as Birch seems to suggest? This is, I think, very improbable, as the right to bear the royal tressure was very jealously restricted : it was very infrequently granted to subjects by the King, and was either a special mark of favour for service done to King or country, or a " Tessera of noble (royal) maternal descent " (Nisbet). This mark of the Scottish Sovereign's favour had its parallel in the " Chief of Empire " (Or, an eagle displayed sable), and in France, " a Chief of France (Azure, semé de lis). It is much more probable that the tressure in both cases is an indication of royal ancestry. Both Kennedy and Graham were grand-sons of King Robert III. Kennedy was the younger son of James Kennedy of Dunnure, by the Lady Mary, Countess of Angus, daughter of Robert III. : Graham was the son of the same Princess, whose third husband was Lord Graham.

(4) On the counter seal of James Beaton, Archbishop of Glasgow, translated to St. Andrews in 1508, there is a saltire of St. Andrew surmounted by a shield bearing quarterly the arms of Beaton and Balfour.

The close connection which existed between the kingdom of Scotland and the diocese of St. Andrews is indicated by the common use of the Bishops on their seals of shields bearing the royal arms. Bishop de Landallis and six other pre-reformation Bishops and Archbishops made use of the royal arms in this way. It was without doubt an allusion to the ancient title, " Bishop of the Scots."

The pre-reformation evidence as to the existence of diocesan arms then is practically negative. With the exception of a few honourable additions to paternal arms on the part of three Bishops, in virtue of their office, or granted to them for other reasons, and the use of the royal arms differenced in allusion to the see, as borne by one Bishop, there is no record of any arms of an official nature. The saltire borne on his seal by Archbishop James Beaton is the nearest approach to the modern arms of the diocese to be found in the seals of the mediæval Bishops.

Of the post-reformation Bishops', there are extant several seals, three of which may be noticed.

(1) George Gladstanes, translated from Caithness in 1606, has left a round seal with a shield bearing a saltire, cantoned in relief with a rose. These arms must not, however, be confounded with those of the diocese: they were the paternal arms of the Bishop, and were used by him also on his official seal as Bishop of Caithness.

(2) Archbishop Sharp bore on his seal the figure of a Bishop holding a crosier in his right hand, and a saltire in the left.

(3) The same device was used by Arthur Ross, the last Archbishop before the disestablishment, and, used as it is apart from the figure of the Apostle, it shows that the saltire of St. Andrew had definitely come to be regarded as the official badge of the see which bore his name.

The arms were in fact recorded by Archbishop Sharp in the Lyon Register, " Azure, a St. Andrew's Cross argent," impaled with the paternal arms of Sharp. This would appear to be conclusive, but apparently there seems to have existed some doubt as to the propriety of the national arms being appropriated as the arms of one particular diocese, because there is a note in the Register as follows :—" Albeit for the seale of the see, he (Sharp) constantly gives, In a field azure, the Image of St. Andrew, the Patron of Scotland, vested and placed within the porch of a church proper, having his crosse of martyrdome on his breast argent, with

these words in flying escrolls on each side, REGI, ECCLESIAE, SACRIS, on the right, and AUSPICE SUMMO NUMINE on the left, and round the seal SIGILLUM ROTUNDUM ARCHIEPISCOPI SANCTI ANDREAE."

This seems to indicate that, though adopted as a badge by the Bishops of the see, the saltire, or national arms of Scotland, could not legitimately be regarded as the official arms of the diocese of St. Andrews. And if such a strong supporter of the Episcopate and of the nexus between church and state as James Sharp, constantly gave the old device of the Bishops' seals as the official diocesan seal—and by giving the tinctures he would seem to wish to extend the use of the device to purposes apart from the seal—there are strong grounds for belief that the diocese of St. Andrews cannot rightly lay claim to the arms at present in use.

But, on the other hand, since from the time of Bishop de Landallis in 1371, the saltire of St. Andrew has been used constantly, practically universally, by the pre-revolution Bishops, in one way or another, either on seals in conjunction with the Apostle, or as a badge, or as a shield of arms, its modern use by their successors, though perhaps not strictly legal, can hardly be regarded as a very heinous offence.

If, however, at any time it should be decided to regularize, so to speak, the heraldry of the Church, it might be well to revert to the device used by at least nineteen pre-revolution Bishops on their seals, namely, St. Andrew on his cross. The shield might be blazoned thus:—"*Azure, the Apostle St. Andrew, vested of the field, surrounded by a radiation or, tied to his cross, argent.*"

The arms in use at present are blazoned thus:—"*Azure, a saltire argent.*"

CHAPTER V.

Dunkeld.

The arms of the diocese of Dunkeld—a Passion cross between two nails—are of comparatively modern origin.

Abernethy and Dunkeld were probably early Columban settlements from the parent house of Iona. About the middle of the ninth century, when the kingdoms of the Scots and the Picts were united under the rule of Kenneth MacAlpin, the king built a new church at Dunkeld, transferred some of the relics of St. Columba to it, and invested Tuathal, Abbat of Dunkeld, as Bishop of Fortrenn, with the primacy of the Pictish church. The translation of the relics from Iona to Dunkeld was probably intended to imply a transference of the primacy—c.f. the translation of the relics of St. Cuthbert from Lindesfarne to Durham. This Bishop Tuathal is called " Primus Episcopus," and Dr Dowden is of the opinion that this means that he was the first Bishop in point of time who exercised Episcopal jurisdiction (The Celtic Church in Scotland) : we have already seen that in former times Bishops in Scotland, as members of a monastic body, took a subordinate position and were subject to the jurisdiction of the Abbat. From now onwards the Bishop of the newly-instituted see began to exercise not only authority as Abbat of the chief Columban house in the country, which contained the relics of the patron, but also as Bishop with a wide and real jurisdiction : he in fact claimed primatial authority over both Picts and

Scots. And this primacy of Dunkeld lasted for many years, until it passed to the " Bishops of the Scots " at St. Andrews.

The cathedral was, as might be expected, from its early history, dedicated to St. Columba, and the effigy of a mitred figure was the prevailing device on the seals of the mediæval Bishops, many of which have come down to our time. As the favourite device on the seals of Bishops of Scottish sees usually had some reference to the patron of the cathedral or diocese, as we have already seen was the custom at St. Andrews, we may infer with some degree of certainty that the figure is intended to represent St. Columba.

There is no doubt as to the identity of the figure depicted on the seals of Bishop Gavin Douglas (1515-1522) and Bishop George Crichton, provided to the see in 1526. On the former of these the figure in a Gothic niche is holding a book in his right hand, on which is perched a dove, and in the latter he is represented holding a dove. The dove was the traditional emblem of St. Columba, whose name signifies Dove.

An interesting seal is that of Bishop John Hamilton (provided 1544). It bears the device of a figure holding a basket with a bird in his right hand. This also is probably intended to represent St. Columba.

The most interesting seal, however, of the mediæval Bishops—from a heraldic point of view—is that of Bishop Nicholas Duffield (1392-1411). The seal bears a figure of the Virgin and Child with a Bishop on each side : above is a representation of the Trinity : in the lower part of the seal is the half figure of a Bishop, on each side of which is a shield : the shield on the dexter side appears to bear "*on a pale a mitre between two doves*": the sinister shield is indecipherable. The charges on this shield, the mitre, and the doves, have the distinct appearance of having been adopted as his arms by Duffield, as the Bishop of a diocese which was under the patronage of St. Columba. As, however, they are not found on the seals of any later Bishops, they cannot be regarded as having been adopted as diocesan arms.

The seal of the cathedral chapter bore on the obverse side a representation of a reliquary, no doubt one of the treasures of the church, in all probability the shrine in which were contained the relics of St. Columba. On its reverse side, the seal bore the figure of the patron.

On some of the mediæval seals, including that of the chapter, there is borne a shield of the royal arms of Scotland. This is no doubt a reference to the primatial dignity of the ancient diocese: we have seen a similar use of the royal arms by the Bishops of St. Andrews, in allusion to the title borne by their predecessors, "Bishop of the Scots."

There is one interesting shield of arms which appears on the seals of two Bishops of Dunkeld, one of whom ruled the see before the reformation, and the other in the 17th century. Both Gavin Douglas, who was consecrated to the diocese in 1516, and Bishop Alexander Lindsay, 1638, bore on their seals the armorial bearings of Abernethy. Bishop Douglas bore these arms as the second quartering on a shield in the base of his seal, and Bishop Lindsay quartered them with the arms of his family. The arms of Abernethy, however, appear as a quartering on the arms of the Lindsays of Evelick, to which branch of the family the Bishop belonged: and probably they are borne on his seal as personal rather than official arms. This seems to be the nearest approach we can find to official armorial bearings in the diocese of Dunkeld before the Revolution. There was from very early times a connection between Abernethy and Dunkeld: in the later days of the Celtic church, the Culdees of Abernethy are said to have claimed the right of appointing the Abbat of Dunkeld. The arms of Abernethy are, "*Or a lion rampant gules, debruised of a ribbon sable.*"

The arms at present in use in the diocese are probably of a conventional nature. The Passion cross may possibly have reference to one of the most prized possessions of the cathedral in the later middle ages: Bishop Lauder, who completed the nave, and executed other works in connection with the building, which he dedicated in 1465, gave many presents to the cathedral, one of which was a silver cross, containing a fragment of the true cross, which was regarded with great veneration.

But this explanation cannot be regarded as satisfactory, and it is far more probable that the arms of the diocese were assumed for no other reason than that they were suitable for ecclesiastical purposes.

They are blazoned thus, "*Argent, a Passion Cross sable, between two nails palewise in base, gules.*"

CHAPTER VI.

Dunblane.

It has already been noted that the practice of using official arms for their dioceses only became general among the Scottish Bishops after the reformation. It was probably the result of the closer intercourse between England and Scotland, consequent on the union of the crowns of the two countries : and this practice was of slow growth, arms being assumed in some dioceses earlier than in others. In fact, the practice never became universal in this country before the church was disestablished. The arms recorded in the Lyon Register, in accordance with the Act of 1672, by James Ramsay, Bishop of Dunblane, are evidence of this : he recorded only his paternal arms, but his successor in the see, Robert Douglas, bore on his seal diocesan arms quartered with his own. As Bishop Douglas only began to rule the see four years before the revolution, it is evident that Dunblane was one of the last of the dioceses to assume arms before the disestablishment of the church. The origin of the arms is not known.

Of the mediæval episcopal seals not many are now in existence. Three of them, those of Bishop Robert de Prebenda, 1258-1282, William, 1284-1293, and Walter de Coventre, provided to the see in 1361, are of interest, as bearing the device of St. Blane or Blaan and St. Lawrence, the patrons of the cathedral. The former of these two saints is said to have been born in Bute in the sixth century :

having been instructed in Ireland by St. Congall and St. Kenneth, he was consecrated Bishop. After a visit to Rome, he returned to Scotland and founded a Columban house at Dunblane, an offshoot of Kingarth in Bute. St. Lawrence may have been St. Augustin's successor at Canterbury : this Lawrence of Canterbury is said to have extended the faith not only among the Angles, but also among the ancient inhabitants of Britain, and even among the Scoti of Ireland : tradition says that he also made a journey to Pictland, and was there visited by St. Ternan, who laboured in the Mearns. Laurencekirk in Forfarshire is a memorial of this traditional friendship, and of the reverence in which the English Archbishop was held in Scotland. Or more probably he was St. Lawrence, the 3rd century Spanish martyr who was roasted to death on a gridiron at Rome. The later mediæval Bishops and chapter in any case identified their patron with the Spanish martyr, as they represent him on their seals holding his traditional emblem, the gridiron on which he suffered death.

The majority of the post-reformation Bishops had no noteworthy device on their episcopal seals—they bore as a rule their paternal arms—but two may be noticed :—

(1) Two seals of Bishop Leighton, 1661-1669. Both of these seals bore the device of a shield charged with the paternal arms of the Bishop, viz., a lion rampant. On one of these seals, which was his official seal as Bishop of Dunblane, above the shield is a mitre and mantling, surmounted by a crest, viz., a lion's head erased, the use of which, as we have already noted, is incorrect in the armorial bearings of a Bishop. The second seal, which is a signet, is on a letter to the Duke of Lauderdale : it shows the shield with a helmet instead of a mitre, together with mantling and crest. The signature of the Bishop on the letter is interesting : he merely

signs R. Leighton, and does not use an official signature derived from his diocese.

(2) Two seals of Bishop Robert Douglas, already referred to, both of which show the arms at present in use in the diocese, in one case quartered, and in the other, as is more usual, impaled with his paternal arms, which are borne with differences on the two seals. This was the first Bishop of Dunblane to use the official armorial bearings of the see.

The arms are blazoned thus:—"*Argent, a Saltire engrailed azure.*"

CHAPTER VII.

Edinburgh.

The arms of the diocese of Edinburgh are derived from those of St. Andrews, as the diocese was formed out of the Archdeaconry of Lothian, hitherto included in the old primatial see of Scotland. Their origin need not be referred to here, as it has already been explained in the chapter dealing with St. Andrews.

The diocese of Edinburgh was founded by King Charles I. in 1663. William Forbes was appointed the first Bishop, and the old Collegiate Church of St. Giles became the cathedral. The diocese still retained some small connection with the parent see, as the Bishop of Edinburgh held the office of Vicar General of the Province of St. Andrews.

The arms—which are unique among those of Scottish dioceses, in that probably they were officially granted by the Lord Lyon—are the same as those of St. Andrews differenced with a mitre in chief. Whether they were actually granted or not to the see, we find them recorded in the Lyon Register by Bishop George Wishart as early as August, 1674.

Bishop Rose, who ruled the see from 1687-1720, bore on his seal a shield of the diocesan arms impaled with his paternal arms : above the shield is a mitre.

These were not, however, the earliest arms of the diocese. A seal of Bishop David Lindsay (1634) bears a shield parted per fess. In the chief a saltire with an open crown in the base for the see of Edinburgh. In the base his paternal arms. Over the shield is an imperial crown, under which is the letter R. No doubt the crowns refer to the royal founder of the see.

It is in one sense a matter of regret, when the arms of the diocese of Edinburgh were first granted or assumed, that, in accordance with the usual Scottish custom, no reference was made in them to local hagiology, though it is true that they are allusive to the patron of the diocese from which the new see was taken. St. Cuthbert, for instance, who had been closely connected with the Lothians and the South-East of Scotland—though his birth-place was still included in the diocese of Glasgow—was one of the most widely venerated of British saints : or again, St. Giles was the traditional patron of Edinburgh and its parish church. Either of these saints or their symbols might have been adopted as armorial bearings of the diocese, in accordance with the general Scottish custom, by which the diocesan arms were derived from the devices allusive to their Patrons borne on their seals by the mediæval Bishops. Or, as the present arms do not appear to have been used before the restoration, it would have been appropriate if they had been made to bear some charge allusive to the founder of the diocese, King Charles the Martyr. And this might even yet be done by adopting Bishop Lindsay's device, and placing a crown in the base of the shield. Thus, while the saltire would still serve to denote the connection between the diocese of Edinburgh and the parent see of St. Andrews, the open crown would be a reminder of the royal founder of the diocese, as well as of the crown of martyrdom which he won.

The arms are blazoned thus :—"*Azure, a Saltire argent, in chief a mitre, garnished or.*"

CHAPTER VIII.

Aberdeen.

The common seal of the city of Aberdeen has had an interesting history. The oldest seal which has come down to us, attached to a charter of 1179, bore on its obverse side a figure of St. Nicholas mitred and his hand raised in benediction. The inscription runs :—" SIGNUM BEATI NICOLAI ABERDONENSIS "; and the reverse side bore the representation of a large church or other building with three spires.

St. Nicholas was the patron saint of the Parish Church of Aberdeen : being regarded as the patron saint of sailors, we often find churches dedicated to him in seaports, e.g., Newcastle and Yarmouth, etc.

The building on the reverse side of the seal was probably a conventional picture of the town, and in all likelihood, the three spires which surmount the building have in process of time developed into the arms, the three towers, which are at present borne by the city. Thus, while the reverse side of the ancient seal has developed into the arms of the city, the obverse side has come to be used as the armorial bearings of the diocese of Aberdeen.

Both devices were recorded for the city in the Lyon Register :—

(1) *Gules, three towers triple-towered, within a double tressure flory counter flory, argent.*

This device, which is universally recognized as the arms of the city need not detain us : it is sufficient to say they appear in their present form as far back as 1520, when they were depicted on the ceiling of St. Machar's Cathedral, and on a seal *ad causas* (1537).

(2) The second blazon contains two errors:—"*Azure a temple argent, St. Michael mitred and vested proper, with his dexter hand lifted up to heaven, praying over three children in a boiling chauldron of the first, and holding in the sinister a crosier, or.*"

The name of Michael is of course a mistake for Nicholas, the patron saint of the town—an Archangel would hardly be represented in episcopal vestments and mitre. The "boiling chauldron" is an incorrect allusion to that miracle of St. Nicholas which was most popular in the Middle Ages:—St. Nicholas was Archbishop of Myra in Cilicia in the fourth century, and the legend relates that during a great famine, the Bishop was travelling through his diocese in order to visit and comfort his people. One night he lodged at an inn, the host of which was a "Son of Satan." This man was in the habit of stealing children, whom he salted, and served up as food to his guests. He set before the Bishop a meal made out of the limbs of three children, but St. Nicholas immediately recognized the nature of the food. Reproaching the inn-keeper for his wickedness, he went to the tub where the remains of the children were being salted, and made the sign of the cross over them. The children immediately sprang up alive and well.

This legend has been sometimes understood to be symbolic of Baptism; the Bishop represents the Church, rescuing souls from death by the saving rite of Baptism; and the inn-keeper is sometimes depicted as a demon with horns and hoofs, and the salting-tub as a font.

A representation of this legend first appears on the seal of the town in 1430, and in it the three children are represented in the tub of the legend. When, however, the arms were recorded in the Lyon Office, this was altered into a "boiling chauldron," and this blazon was retained by Woodward in the arms of the diocese of Aberdeen.

It was probably from this legend that St. Nicholas came to be venerated as the patron saint of children—especially schoolboys—and in this character he annually comes on Christmas Eve under the guise of Santa Claus, i.e., Nicholas. He died in 326 or 342 on December 6th, and was buried at Bari in Apulia.

The seals of the mediæval Bishops, though interesting as bearing for the most part, shields charged with their paternal arms, have no bearing on the arms at present in use in the diocese. The prevailing device on the main part of the shield was the Virgin and Child, Old Aberdeen being under the protection of St. Mary, to whom King's College was dedicated.

The seal of Bishop Gavin Dunbar, however, is of interest, as introducing St. Nicholas. This Saint is depicted on the right of the Virgin Mary, while a Bishop (? Machar) stands on the left.

The seal of the cathedral chapter also is worthy of notice. It bore on the upper part a figure of the Virgin and Child under a Gothic niche : the lower part of the seal is divided into three niches, in the centre one of which is the figure of a Bishop, which Laing thinks may be intended for St. Nicholas : but it is as likely, if not more so, that it was meant for St. Machar, the traditional founder of the old diocese, who built the first church, in accordance with the directions of St. Columba, at the place where a river took the form of a pastoral staff—the site of the mediæval cathedral on the banks of the River Don.

The seals of the post-reformation Bishops also present no particular interest, and have no bearing on the modern arms of the see.

We can find, then, practically no trace of the diocesan arms in the ancient ecclesiastical records, and they must be regarded as having been derived from the common seal of the cathedral city, as we shall find was also the case with the diocesan arms of Moray.

But, although, of course, there is no authority for their use by the diocese of Aberdeen, they are by no means inappropriate, and there can be little objection to their being retained : in fact, they serve a useful purpose by preserving the memory of the device borne on one side of the ancient seal of the city, while the city arms keep alive the memory of the other.

In the picture of the shield, reproduced above, it should be noticed that the "Temple"—which represents the architectural canopy over the saint in the seals—is drawn in the Byzantine style in allusion to the locality of the diocese which St. Nicholas ruled. The saint himself is drawn "in pontificals," i.e., vested in the conventional robes of a Bishop, in alb, chasuble, and mitre. Lord Bute, in discussing the arms of the city of Aberdeen, urges that the saint should be vested in the distinctive robes of an Eastern Bishop. In heraldry, however, there is a traditional manner of representing a Bishop, to which it is best to adhere, and all the more so as the robes of a fourth century Eastern Bishop must be more or less a matter of conjecture.

The arms of the diocese may be blazoned thus :— "*Azure, in the porch of a Temple argent, St. Nicholas standing mitred and vested proper, holding in his sinister hand a crosier or, with his dexter hand lifted up to heaven, praying over three children proper in a salting-tub of the field.*"

CHAPTER IX.

Orkney.

The arms of the diocese of Orkney bear the figure of St. Magnus, the patron of the see and of the cathedral at Kirkwall.

Orkney and Zetland were early colonized by Scandinavians, whose influence gradually spread throughout the Hebrides also. These colonists were in the habit of making raids on the coasts of Britain, and they even sent expeditions against Norway itself. In the tenth century Harold, King of Norway, sailed to the Western seas and annexed the Orkneys and the Hebrides, and over these islands he placed Norwegian Earls as governors. They and their descendants ruled for some centuries, nominally as vassals of the kings of Norway, but generally, to all intents and purposes, independent sovereigns. Magnus was the son of Erlend, one of the Scandinavian Earls of Orkney. He was one of a family, the members of which were continually quarrelling among themselves, and stirring up strife in the islands; and, to restore order, Magnus Barefoot, King of Norway, came to Orkney in the year 1098. He sent the two Earls, Erlend and Paul, his brother, back to Norway as prisoners. He then took Magnus and his brother, the younger Erlend, and their cousin Haco, the son of Paul, on a marauding expedition round the West of Scotland. They penetrated as far as Anglesea, where a battle was fought with the Norman earls of Chester and

Shrewsbury. The young Magnus refused to take any part in the battle, because, as he said in answer to the angry enquiry of the king, " No man here has done me wrong, and therefore I will not fight " : he is said to have recited the psalter as long as the battle lasted. After the death of his brother in Ireland in 1102, his father and uncle having died in Norway, Magnus was invested with the Earldom of Caithness, and it is recorded that his just government and holy life gained him the reverence and affection of all his subjects. Meanwhile his cousin Haco had seized the Earldom of Orkney, but on appeal to the King of Norway, Magnus received his father's half. For two years the cousins ruled in comparative harmony, but the old family dissensions broke out again, and eventually brought about the murder of Magnus by his cousin. The two earls agreed to meet in battle at Eglishay with an equal number of ships and retainers; Haco, however, treacherously arrived with eight ships instead of two, which was the number arranged. His followers were prepared to fight for Magnus, but he refused to endanger the lives of his friends, and declined the unequal battle. He knew well that his life was in imminent danger, and he spent the night in the church, and in the morning received the Blessed Sacrament : the followers of Haco entered the building, and seized Magnus, and he was condemned to death. He kneeled, confessing his sins, and praying for his murderers. He then signed himself with the sign of the cross, and bending forward, his head fell at the second stroke of the executioner's sword. He was afterwards buried at Christ Church, Birsa, by his mother Thora. Almost immediately after his death men began to venerate him as a saint, and when in 1138 his nephew Earl Ronald began to build the cathedral of Kirkwall, it was dedicated in the name of St. Magnus, and his relics were removed to the building which has since borne his name.

During the middle ages St. Magnus was held in great reverence in the Northern Islands, and as might be expected, his effigy finds a place among the devices on the seals which have come down to us. Unfortunately not many of the mediæval seals have survived, but two of them are of interest to us.

The seal of Bishop de Tulloch, 1422, bears a representation of St. Magnus holding a sword, as does that of Adam Bothwell, 1559.

The chapter seal of Kirkwall cathedral bore the design of a Gothic porch of a centre and two side doors : in the centre is the figure of the patron holding a sword in his right hand : and in the side doors are figures of monks in prayer.

But although the information to be obtained from the mediæval seals is very meagre, there are other indications of the close traditional connection of St. Magnus with the diocese of Orkney. Bishop Maxwell gave a peal of bells to the cathedral in 1528, and three of the bells bear a medallion, showing a representation of St. Magnus holding a sword. And on the Archdeaconry at Kirkwall, there are the sculptured remains of the arms of Archdeacon Fulzie (1566) with the device of a crown, which may be an allusion to the royal saint.

Of the post-reformation Bishops, Andrew Honeyman, 1664, has left a seal, in some ways not unlike that of the mediæval chapter, showing St. Magnus in the centre niche of three, holding in his hand what appears to be a crozier, but may have been intended for the usual sword, or perhaps a sceptre. On the arch of the middle niche is inscribed S. MAGNVS.

The saint, although in reality his title was that of Earl of Orkney, is as a rule represented as a king, crowned, and holding a sword in his right hand, no doubt in allusion to his death.

The arms of the diocese then trace their origin to the saint who gave his name to the cathedral of Kirkwall. And although St. Magnus was not in himself a particularly striking figure, the arms are appropriate and interesting in their allusion to a past epoch in Scottish history, when the Northern islands were under the sway of the King of Norway, and the diocese of Orkney was under the jurisdiction of the Archbishop of Trondhjem.

The arms are blazoned:—"*Argent, St. Magnus, standing, royally vested, on his head a crown of gold, in his dexter hand a sword, proper.*"

CHAPTER X.

Moray.

The arms of the diocese of Moray, like those of Aberdeen, are derived not from the dedication of the cathedral, as is common in Scotland, but from that of the parish church of the cathedral city. The diocesan arms of Moray are in fact nothing more than an adaptation of the Common Seal of the Burgh of Elgin.

They represent St. Giles or Aegidius standing in a church porch, holding in his right hand a cross, and in his left a book. It would be correct to depict, in addition, a hind pierced in the back with an arrow fawning against him: The hind is so generally connected with St. Giles (cf., the Supporters in the arms of the City of Edinburgh), that even though not mentioned in the blazon of the shield, it may be considered an integral part of the heraldic representation of the Saint.

St. Giles was an Athenian of the 8th century, who, becoming celebrated for his charity and his miraculous gifts of healing, and fearing that the resulting fame would endanger his soul, retired from his native country to a remote cave in the neighbourhood of Nimes in France, where he lived as a hermit on wild herbs and the milk of a hind. One day the King of France—so runs the legend—who was hunting in the neighbourhood, shot the hind, wounding it. He followed it and came to St. Giles' retreat, where he found the Saint holding the wounded hind in his arms. The King, recognising that he was a man of God, entreated him to allow a monastery to be built in the place where his cave was. This was done, and St. Giles, at the request of the King, became Abbat of the monastery, which he is said to have ruled " wisely and Godly for some years, until he passed away to heaven."

The " church porch " in the shield is merely the architectural canopy under which the Saint was depicted on the ancient Burgh seals, but in its Gothic appearance it is by no means inappropriate when we remember the connection between St. Giles and the great monastery which bore his name and of which tradition says he was the first Abbat.

In the episcopal records of the see we can find no trace of St. Giles. There are extant the seals of sixteen Bishops, fourteen of whom governed the diocese before the Reformation. Of these nine show their paternal arms. Bishop John Pilmore in 1357 bore on his seal, in addition to his paternal arms, a shield charged with the arms of the province of Moray, viz., 3 cushions within a double tressure flory counter flory. This is the sole case of any approach to official arms on the part of the Bishops of Moray, and was used only to indicate the extent of the diocese. The prevailing device, which occurs on the seals of nine (possibly ten) pre-reformation Bishops, was a representation of the Holy Trinity, which was the dedication of the Cathedral at Elgin. The two post-reformation Bishops, whose seals are extant, bore their paternal arms, and one of them, Bishop John Guthrie, in 1623, on his seal revived the old device of a representation of the Holy Trinity, flanked on either side respectively by the Blessed Virgin and St. Michael.

But although among the episcopal seals of Moray we can find no trace of St. Giles, on the seal of the Cathedral Chapter there is the rude figure of a saint holding a book in his left hand : this saint has not been identified, but from the fact that he holds a book in the left hand it is possible that the figure represents St. Giles. Both in the Burgh seal of Elgin (copied in the modern diocesan arms of Moray), and in the seal of the Chapter of St. Giles at Edinburgh (1496), the saint is represented as holding a book in his left hand. So possibly the book held in the left hand may identify the figure on the Chapter seal of Elgin with St. Giles. But this is only conjecture, and nothing should be deduced as a certainty from this seal.

The arms then at present used in the diocese of Moray cannot claim any ancient authority as diocesan arms, but they nevertheless have a distinct historical value. And their value consists in this:—Depicting, as they do, the patron saint of the ancient Cathedral city, they serve to emphasise the identity of the modern diocese of Moray with its Cathedral at Inverness, with the ancient and mediæval diocese with its Cathedral at St. Giles' town of Elgin.

The arms may be blazoned thus:—"*Azure, within a Church Porch St. Giles, vested and mitred, holding in his dexter hand a Cross, and in the sinister a Book; fawning against him a Hind pierced in the back by an arrow, all proper.*"

CHAPTER XI.

Ross.

In March, 1673, John Paterson, Bishop of Ross, in accordance with the act of the previous year, recorded at the Lyon Office the arms which are still in use as the official arms of the diocese: but although he was careful to carry out the requirements of the law, he does not appear to have understood the significance of the arms which had been officially used by at least one of his predecessors.

The arms represent two figures:—Dexter, a saint in a red garment, his hands folded on his breast; sinister, a Bishop. Bishop Paterson recorded these arms with the Lyon as follows:—"*Argent, a Bishop standing on the sinister habited in a long robe close girt, purpure, mitred, and holding in his left hand a crosier or, and pointing with his right to St. Boniface on the dexter side, clothed, and both his hands laid on his breast, proper.*" This interpretation has been accepted by Woodward, and has been retained in the Church Year Book. Now, in naming the dexter figure St. Boniface, Bishop Paterson was, I think, in error: it had evidently been forgotten who the other figure was intended to represent, and probably no investigation was made as to the origin of the arms: and for this we must look in the history of the Cathedral of the Diocese.

The first Cathedral of the see was erected at Rosemarkie by St. Boniface or Quiritinus in the seventh century, and was dedicated to St. Peter. Boniface was one of the many semi-legendary early Scottish churchmen—though he was Scottish only by adoption and not by birth—and, of course, must not be confounded with Boniface, the Englishman, who became Archbishop of Mainz and Apostle of Germany. The legend of St. Boniface in the Breviary of Aberdeen, though containing some obvious historic errors, relates some facts for the accuracy of which there is a certain amount of circumstantial evidence. Nectan, King of Pictavia, who has been described as a King of Romanizing tendencies, sent to Rome for clergy to counteract and overcome the influence of the Columban missionaries in his kingdom. The Aberdeen Breviary relates that *Pope* Boniface came to Scotland with some companions whose names are given; Nectan and his whole court were baptized, and Boniface and his companions set to work to evangelize the country. Though the title of Pope is clearly incorrect, there are three facts which tend to confirm the truth of the journey of Boniface and its object, and his subsequent labours:—

(1) Many ancient church dedications in the district covered by his labours bear the names of the reputed companions of his mission, as Benedict, Madianus, Servanus, Pensandus, and Triduana.

(2) The dedication of his cathedral is significant, and the number of churches dedicated to St. Peter in the district is in favour of the view that he was a *Roman* Missionary who came to bring the local church into conformity with the see of St. Peter.

(3) On one of the seals of the Burgh of Fortrose, where the later cathedral was built, Boniface is depicted holding a key probably to emphasize the fact that it was the Roman Church of which he was the representative, which held the keys of the Kingdom of God.

Probably in 1235 the seat of the Bishop was transferred to the neighbouring town of Fortrose, and the new cathedral was dedicated to St. Peter and St. Boniface, the patron and the founder of the ancient cathedral.

We see then that two names were held up to special reverence in the district which in the ecclesiastical organization of Scotland came to be known as the Diocese of Ross, St. Peter the Apostle and St. Boniface; and we shall not be out of our reckoning if we identify the two figures on the present diocesan arms with these two saints.

We may now turn to the development of the arms. Of the pre-Reformation Bishops, not many seals remain extant, and these show no prevailing device : several Bishops bore their paternal arms. Two (Roger, or Robert, in 1304, and Alexander Steward, provided 1350) bore the arms of the province of Ross, viz., three lions rampant (in the case of Alexander within the royal tressure), in allusion, of course, to the territory over which they held spiritual authority. Bishop Robert, 1253-1270, showed on the reverse side of his seal a bust of a Bishop in pontificals, with the inscription : " SCS. BONIFATIUS." Bishop John Fraser or Frisel, 1498, on his seal showed St. Peter with the keys and a cross, and Bishop Robert, 1280-1296, showed St. Peter and St. Boniface within two Gothic niches. The Chapter seal bore the figures of the same two Saints, with the inscription : " SIGILLUM CAPITULI SANCTORUM PETRI ET BONIFACII DE ROSMARKIN."

Of the post-Reformation Bishops, John Maxwell in 1635 bore on his seal a shield bearing the two figures, assumed as the arms of the diocese impaled with his paternal arms : this is the first appearance, as far as we know, of the device of the two saints as the definitely official arms of the see, which were afterwards recorded by Bishop Paterson in the Lyon Register in 1673.

Another question now arises : we have identified the two figures as St. Peter and St. Boniface, but which is St. Boniface and which is St. Peter? In spite of Bishop Paterson, I think there can be no doubt that the Bishop represents the former, and the Saint described in the Register as "*clothed and both his hands laid on his breast,*" i.e., the dexter figure, the latter. Four facts support this view :—

(1) The dexter being the more honourable side, it would naturally be assigned to St. Peter, not only as the earlier patron of the see, but also as the Prince of the Apostles.

(2) St. Peter would not be depicted in mediæval Heraldry—or indeed elsewhere—as a Bishop; while it would be extremely improbable that the traditional founder of a see would be depicted in any other manner on diocesan seals, etc.

(3) The colour of the robe of the dexter figure seems to indicate St. Peter. It is usually blazoned gules : and, though the colours of St. Peter are as a rule blue and yellow, the red robe would here be used with reference to his martyrdom; whereas St. Boniface, as far as is known, did not die a martyr's death, so we would expect his colour to be either white or the episcopal purple; and the sinister figure on the shield is vested purpure.

(4) On the seal of Bishop Robert 2nd, already referred to, the episcopally vested figure is expressly named Scs. Bonifatius.

The only variation of the diocesan arms is that used by Bishop James Ramsay (1684). He bore on his episcopal seal a shield charged with one figure, St. Peter, for the see of Ross, quartered with his paternal arms.

The arms of the diocese of Ross should be blazoned thus, "*Argent, on the sinister side, St. Boniface, pontifically vested purpure, mitred and holding in his left hand a crozier or, and pointing with his right to St. Peter on the dexter side, habited gules, and both his hands laid on his breast.*"

CHAPTER XII.

Caithness.

The arms of the diocese of Caithness are of comparatively modern origin, and cannot be regarded as very satisfactory, being merely of a conventional nature. They have no particular connection with the diocese or its history; the couped saltires have a rather insignificant appearance, and have no traditional or heraldic connection with the Crown of Thorns. This is the more unfortunate, as in the few seals of the mediæval Bishops which have come down to us—and most of them have only come to light in recent years—there are some of great heraldic interest : one of them in particular would have afforded a far more satisfactory basis on which the armorial bearings of the diocese might have been formed.

Three of the mediæval seals are of particular interest to us :—

(1) That of William, who was Bishop of the diocese in 1250. His seal bore the device of a Bishop in a boat as seen from the prow, his hands held up in adoration. This may possibly refer to one of the miracles of his predecessor in the see, St. Gilbert, who was, by the way, the last Scot to be venerated as a Saint.

Gilbert, Archdeacon of Moray, became Bishop of Caithness about the year 1223. He was evidently a man of great ability and force of character, and ruled his turbulent diocese for about twenty years. Among other works he rebuilt the cathedral of Dornoch, the dedication of which was St. Mary, labouring with his own hands. He found it a small church served by one priest; he left it with a full chapter, and statutes based on those of Elgin, which had in turn been derived from Lincoln.

The legend already referred to, is as follows:—
"A certain person had hired the salmon fishings from the Lord of Caithness for a sum of money. Owing to the lack of fish, he had not wherewithal to pay his rent, and when the season arrived, that it might not pass without profit, he earnestly besought Bishop Gilbert to wash his holy hands in the water, and so attract the salmon, which accordingly took place." (Forbes, "Calendars of Scottish Saints.") After his death in 1245, Gilbert became patron of the diocese and cathedral.

(2) Bishop Thomas Murray de Fingask, consecrated 1343, bore on his seal the device of a Bishop between two shields; the dexter shield bearing the paternal arms of Murray, and the sinister, a Lymphad or Galley within a double tressure, flory counter flory. The latter shield is something of a mystery. The arms are those of the Lord of the Isles, and the inscription on the seal as read by Laing is " S. THOME DEI GRA EPI CATHENENSIS ET INSULA," the seal of Thomas, Bishop of Caithness and the Isles. Laing therefore regarded this shield as having been borne on his seal by Bishop Murray in allusion to his see of the Isles, the arms of the Earldom of Caithness being a galley or lymphad without the tressure. There is, however, no record of this Bishop having held the see of the Isles in addition to Caithness, and according to Woodward the shield is intended to allude to the latter diocese.

A later writer on Scottish seals (McDonald, "Scottish Armorial Seals") throws new light on the ques-

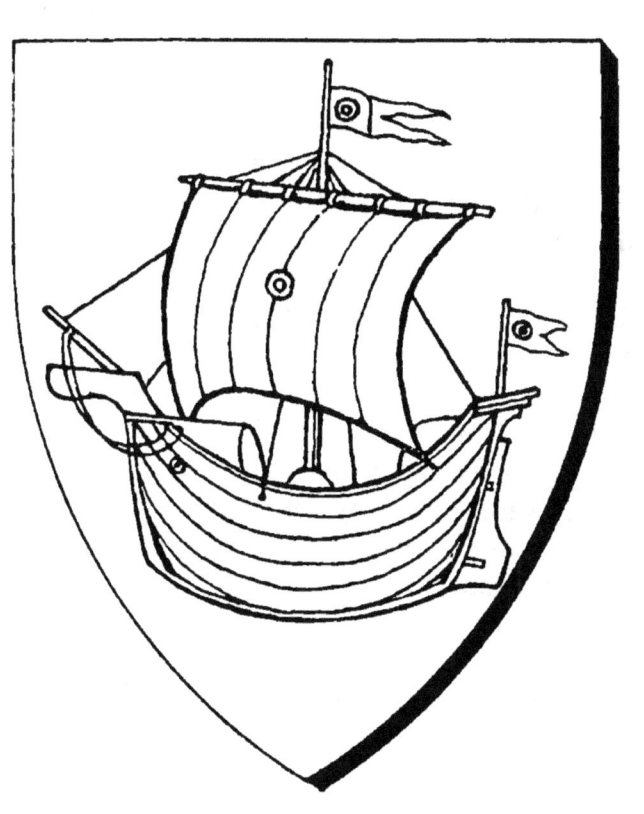

tion. He reads the inscription : "S. THOME DEI GRA EPI CATHENENSIS IN SCOCIA." The shield therefore would thus appear without doubt to be intended for the diocese of Caithness.

But the tressure still presents a difficulty. Lindsay of the Mount, Burke, and others all agree in blazoning the arms of the Earldom of Caithness as "a galley in full sail"—no tressure. But though as a general rule the galley is blazoned without the tressure, on the seal of John, Earl of Caithness (1296), there is a shield charged with a galley within the royal tressure, so the use of this device was not unknown.

It may therefore be assumed that the shield on Bishop Murray's seal is intended to represent the arms of the Earldom of Caithness; and that for some reason, unknown to us, the shield was charged with the honourable addition of the royal tressure.

(3) The arms of the province of Caithness, as already noted, were a galley in full sail, and this device appears as quarterings on the seal of Bishop Andrew Stuart I., who was provided to the see in 1501. He differenced the arms of the province with an annulet (a plain ring) in the fess point of the shield (i.e., the central point of the shield). In England the annulet was the difference customarily borne on the family arms by the fifth son, but as Bishop Stuart was an illegitimate son of the house of Invermeath, the annulet would not have been used here in this connection. It was perhaps borne by the Bishop to differentiate between the arms of the "Bishop" and those of the "Earl" of Caithness.

The post-reformation Bishops bore on their seals their family arms, and they are of no particular interest.

It should be noted then that in the past records of the

see, at any rate as far as the Bishops are concerned, the favourite device, as far as we know, was allusive to the sea and ships.

Now the modern arms are without authority: they have not yet been long enough in actual use to become traditionally identified with the diocese, as is the case with the arms of Dunblane for instance, which, like those of Caithness, have never been recorded at the Lyon Office: the combination of saltires and Crown of Thorns has no significance, and the sizes of the tiny saltires and the comparatively gigantic Crown, are out of all proportion to one another.

On the other hand the shield borne by Bishop Andrew Stuart, the golden galley with a silver sail on an azure ground, an annulet depicted on the sail, would be in every way a satisfactory shield of arms for the see. Not only is it derived from the arms of the province from which the diocese takes its name, but the galley is a device of great beauty, and very characteristic of Scottish Heraldry: it is appropriate too for a diocese which is almost surrounded by the sea. It is also ecclesiastically appropriate—the ship of the church, bearing the ring, the symbol of eternity.

Would it then be too much to hope that the present armorial bearings of the diocese of Caithness might be abandoned in favour of the ancient, beautiful, and appropriate device, "*Azure, a Galley, or, in full sail, argent, bearing on its sail, and flying on flag and pennon, an annulet of the field.*"

The arms at present in use are blazoned thus:—"*Azure, a Crown of Thorns or, between three Saltires couped, argent.*"

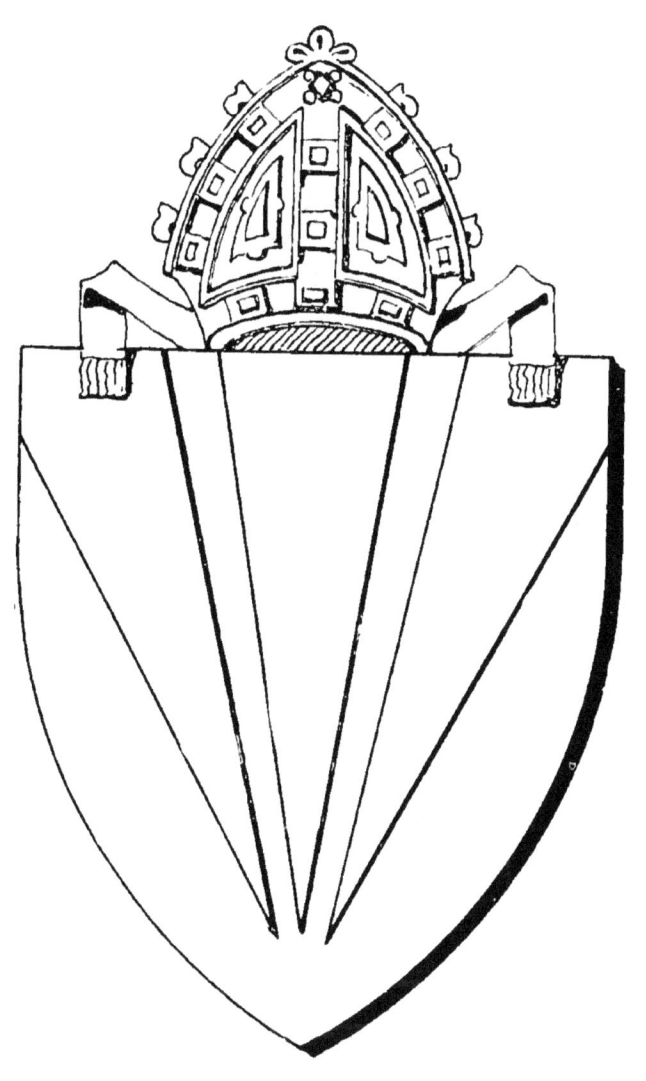

CHAPTER XIII.

Brechin.

The diocese of Brechin has the honour of sharing its armorial bearings with the Crown. The three piles in point were blazoned on the arms of Henry de Brechin, natural son of David, Earl of Huntingdon in England, and Earl of Garioch and Lord of Brechin in Scotland, half brother of William the Lion. He took his surname from the Lordship of Brechin, which he obtained from his father. After some vicissitudes the lands passed to the Earls of Dalhousie, and the Lordship was annexed to the Crown in 1437.

The arms of the see, as we shall find in the case of Glasgow also, are identical with those of the cathedral city, the little town being no doubt a mere adjunct of the cathedral.

At Brechin we find that there has existed a certain amount of confusion as to the correct blazoning of the arms of the city and diocese. Three different varieties of armorial bearings have been used at different times as the offcial arms :—-

> (1) The Cathedral of Brechin was dedicated to the Holy Trinity, and on the seals of the mediæval Bishops the prevailing device was a pictorial representation of the Trinity. The earliest Bishops whose seals have come down to us show, as might be expected, a simpler device, but from the time of Bishop Patrick de Locrys (Leuchars), who ruled over the diocese from 1351 until his resignation in 1383, every Bishop whose seal survives, with the possible exception of George

de Schoreswood, 1453/4-1462, bore a representation of the Trinity. The mediæval draughtsmen did not scruple to draw the Eternal Father, usually represented as a venerable Man in a long robe, supporting between his knees the crucified Son, while the Holy Spirit, in the form of a Dove, is also depicted.

Thomas Meldrum, Official of the diocese, 1514, bore on his seal a representation of the Trinity, and the same device was used on the seal of the cathedral chapter; on the latter the Holy Spirit is shown descending from the Father to the Son. (1509).

The city bore practically the same device, which in Burke's "General Armory" is quaintly blazoned, "Or, a representation of the Trinity, proper"!

(2) Of the post-reformation Bishops, two retained on their shields the device used by their predecessors in the middle ages, but three of them, David Strachan, 1662, George Haliburton, 1678, and James Drummond, 1684, showed the figure of a Bishop with uplifted hands: Bishop Haliburton bore this device on a shield impaled with his paternal arms, and Laing takes it to be the armorial bearings assumed for the see.

Now the arms of the city have been blazoned:— "*Azure, in the porch of a Gothic church, its lower extremity terminating in the nombril point, argent, a saint sitting, proper, habited of the field; in base an escutcheon of the second charged with three piles issuing from the chief and meeting in the base point, gules.*" (Cumming MS.); and Black in his "History of Brechin to 1864" identifies the saint borne on the arms of the town as St. Ninian.

The seal also of a 14th century Official of the diocese bore the head of a mitred Bishop, which may possibly be intended to represent the same saint.

(3) The arms at present in use, "*Or, three piles in point, gules.*" These were originally, as we have already seen, the arms of Henry de Brechin, son of the Earl of Huntingdon, and in the course of time they have come to be borne by the diocese and town of Brechin. In Burke's "Armory" they are given in addition to his blazon of the Trinity; and in the description of the town arms in the Cumming MS. these bearings are borne on an escutcheon in the base of the shield. They are also found on various churches of the diocese; for instance, they are carved on the west side of the old church tower at Dundee: and over the window in the remains of the ancient church of Mains in Forfarshire there is a sculptured fragment, representing the Annunciation, and, below a pot of lilies, is a shield bearing two piles in point (the third pile has been lost).

Now, how are we to reconcile these three different armorial bearings? First as regards (2), St. Ninian had no connection with Brechin, and it is difficult to guess why he should have been depicted as the armorial bearings of the town and diocese. Probably the episcopal figure referred to on the seals of the post-reformation Bishops is not to be regarded as anything more than the conventional figure borne universally by the earliest Bishops, whose seals have come down to us, and need not be identified at all.

As regards (3), we may gain some light from the cathedral which was dedicated to the Holy Trinity. In the majority of the Scottish sees the diocesan arms are derived from the patron of the cathedral, either in the shape of an effigy of the saint himself, or as a pictorial representation of one of his miracles; we have already seen that the practically universal device borne on the seals of the mediæval Bishops of Brechin was a pictorial representation of the Holy Trinity.

Bearing these two facts in mind, we may now try to determine the significance of the charge, three piles in point. The piles have been supposed to represent passion nails; but there seems to be no good reason for this explanation of the charge. The nails could hardly have altered so much from their original shape, as we may see them depicted on the arms of the diocese of Dunkeld : so we must look for another explanation of the three piles in point.

Now " three," when we remember the dedication of the cathedral suggests the Trinity, and " In point," the three all meeting and converging in one, again is suggestive of the Trinity. Lord Bute has put forward the theory that these three piles in point are a heraldic translation of the actual picture which was borne on the seals of the Bishops and others in earlier times. He takes the three piles to be three broadening rays of light proceeding from one point, and this explanation has much to support it. It connects the charge with the prevailing device on the seals of the Bishops, and also with the dedication of the cathedral. The arms were first assumed by David, Earl of Huntingdon, who was born in 1143, and the cathedral of Brechin was founded in 1150, but, as Lord Bute points out, " We have not sufficient knowledge to enable us to suggest either that the dedication was derived from them, or that they were taken from the dedication." (The arms of the Royal and Parliamentary Burghs of Scotland.) In either case, the probabilities are that there was some connection between the cathedral of Brechin and the arms of the Lordship, which were afterwards assumed by the town and diocese, and that they represent heraldically the Holy Trinity, which reverence forbids men to depict in any but a symbolic manner.*

We may repeat the blazon of the arms thus :—" *Or, three Piles in point, gules.*"

*It is not intended that the reader should understand that the not uncommon charge of " three piles in point " always or even generally refers to the Trinity : but that in this case the charge may have had some relationship to the Dedication of Brechin Cathedral.

CHAPTER XIV.

Glasgow.

Of the many interesting armorial bearings of Scotland, there are none better known than those of the city and diocese of Glasgow.

> This is the tree that never grew,
> This is the bird that never flew,
> This is the fish that never swam,
> And this is the bell that never rang.

So runs one version of the rhyme, the popularity of which indicates the general interest taken in these arms even by people who, as a rule, pay no attention to the science of heraldry.

The origin of these arms has been the subject of much discussion, and their derivation has been found in different sources. The arms were not recorded till the year 1866 by the Town Council of Glasgow, though they had been in use for a long time previously. The arms as used by the diocese of Glasgow were never registered, and are identical with those of the city: they are, however, not to be regarded as having been "borrowed" from the city, as was done in the case of the sees of Aberdeen and Moray; in Glasgow the contrary was the case, as it was the city which derived its arms from devices borne on the seals of the mediæval Bishops.

Of the different interpretations which have been given to the arms, we may mention four :—

(1) That offered by Dr Eyre, late Roman Catholic Archbishop of Glasgow. He suggests that the four emblems, the fish, the tree, the bird, and the bell, are used in allusion to St. Kentigern and his work. The fish is symbolic of the office to which he, like the Apostles, was called, to become a fisher of men, the ring in its mouth being the usual symbol of immortality. The tree refers to the church of Kentigern, which grew from small beginnings to great dimensions, like the mustard seed in the Parable; and the redbreast is representative of the birds of the air which should come and lodge in the branches. The bell is an allusion to the world-wide fame of the saint, "Yes, verily, their sound went unto all the earth, and their words unto the ends of the world."

(2) Cleland in his "Annals" (1828), appendix, quoted in the "Book of Glasgow Cathedral," gives the following explanation :—" The tree is emblematical of the spreading of the Gospel, its leaves being represented as for the healing of the nations. The bird is also typical of that glorious event, so beautifully described under the similitude of the winter being past, and the rain over and gone, and the time of the singing of birds being come. Bells for calling the faithful to prayers were considered so important in matters of religion, that the rite of consecration was conferred on them by the dignitaries of the Roman Church. As to the salmon, it may refer to a tradition . . . . of St. Mungo (this will be referred to later), in the year 600: or it may have reference to the staple trade of the town, which was fishing and curing salmon from a very early period. . . . . "

(3) Dr Arthur Johnstoun in 1642 published an epigram

relating to the arms of the city of Glasgow,
"Insignia Civitatis Glasguae": this was translated
forty years later by John Barclay, Minister of
Cruden, and published at Aberdeen :—

The SALMON which a *Fish* is of the *Sea*,
The OAK which springs from *Earth*, that *loftie Tree*,
The BIRD on it, which in the *Air* doth flee,
O GLASGOW, does presage all things to thee.
To which the *Sea* or *Air* or *Fertile Earth*
Do either give their *Nourishment* or *Birth*.
The BELL that doth to *Public Worship* call
Sayes HEAVEN will give most lasting things of all.
The RING the token of the *Marriage* is
Of things in *Heav'n* and *Earth* both thee to bless.

These three explanations rest on no evidence, but are based on conjecture. The fourth interpretation has the support of tradition, as well as of the devices on the seals of the mediæval Bishops :—

(4) According to tradition, the armorial bearings of Glasgow are derived from incidents in the life of St. Kentigern or Mungo, the Founder and first Bishop of the ancient see.

Kentigern, as is well known, was the illegitimate son of the Christian Thenew (Enoch), a Pictish Princess whose home was at Traprain in the district now known as East Lothian. According to the tribal custom, as a punishment for inchastity, she was set adrift in an open boat at Aberlady, and is said to have been carried by the tides and winds outside the May Island, and then up the Forth to the shore of Culross, where the mother and the newly-born child were taken under the protection of St. Serf. The child received the name of Kentigern (? Chief Lord), and grew up under the care of St. Serf, to whom he so endeared himself that he gave him the name of Mungo or Dear One. It was at this period of his life that he worked the miracles connected with the bird and the tree. The bird was a pet robin of St. Serf; the legend, as related in Joceline's Life of St. Kentigern, tells how in the absence of St. Serf in church, his pupils were playing with the bird, and in the struggle as to who should have it, unfortunately pulled its head off: they then laid the blame on Kentigern, who at once restored it to life by prayer and the sign of the cross. The tree was originally a branch of hazel: the boys in St. Serf's school were responsible, each one for a week at a time, for keeping in order the fire from which the church lights were kindled. Kentigern's enemies maliciously extinguished the fire, when he was in charge, but he rekindled it with a branch of hazel which miraculously burst into flame.—This was, in more ways than one, a miraculous branch, as it has since grown not only into a tree, but into an oak tree, under which guise it is recorded in the Lyon office for the City of Glasgow.

While still a young man, Kentigern came to Cathures, the modern Glasgow, and began to preach the Gospel beside the Molendinar Burn, where, according to tradition, St. Ninian had consecrated a cemetery, and he was chosen as Bishop by the Prince of Strathclyde. Later in life, he was forced by the Pagan party to flee the country; he went to Wales, where he spent some years with St. David, and is said to have founded the diocese of St. Asaph. He at last returned to his old diocese of Strathclyde, and in this later period he worked the miracle which has left its record in the salmon and ring on the shield of arms of Glasgow. Queen Langueth, of Cadzow, having a young lover at the court, gave him a ring which had been a gift to her from her husband. The king, hearing of this, managed, when the young man was asleep, to draw the ring from his finger, and threw it into the Clyde. He then returned home, and asked his wife to show him the ring. Of course she was unable to produce it, and the king gave her three days in which to find it. The queen, in despair, sent a messenger with an urgent entreaty for help to St. Mungo, who bade him throw a line and hook into the river : he did so, and caught a salmon, in which was found the queen's ring. When the king again demanded to see the ring, it was duly produced, and his suspicions were set at rest. The queen is said to have amended her life at the exhortations of the saint. He died about the year 600, and probably his body still rests under the cathedral at Glasgow which bears his name.

The bell is supposed to represent that of St. Kentigern, which, according to a not very reliable tradition, had been a gift from the Pope. He is said to have hung it on a tree beside the Molendinar Burn, and to have used it at service time. In any case, bells of a quadrangular shape figure largely among Celtic ecclesiastical antiquities : we shall hear of another bell in connection with St. Moluag of Lismore. After the Reformation St. Mungo's bell fell into the hands of two citizens, who on November 19th, 1577, sold it to the Town Council. £10 was paid for the bell, and there is a record of the Council, " Andro (Laing) to be maid burges gratis . . . for ye said caus of ye bell." It was used by the city bellringer as late as 1661, but is now lost.

I have already noted that the first three explanations rest on nothing more substantial than conjecture, but the traditional derivation—and the fact that it rests on popular tradition, in a case of this sort is an argument in favour of its correctness—is supported by the devices on the seals of the mediæval Bishops.

Many of these seals survive, and twelve of them bear the device of the salmon and the ring. John de Lindesay, consecrated 1323, bore the redbreast as well as the salmon. The chapter seal (1321) and the seal of the Official of the diocese (1523) both bore the bell.

The most interesting from our point of view of the series of Bishops' seals, are two of Robert Wischard, consecrated 1273.

The first is an early seal, and represents St. Mungo in the act of benediction: on the dexter side is a bird on a branch; on the sinister, a salmon holding a ring. Here we have the earliest representation of the " tree."

The other seal (1315) is divided horizontally into three parts. The upper compartment shows a monk kneeling and presenting a fish with a ring to St. Mungo, who is sitting. In the middle division there are two niches: in the dexter, a figure holding a sword in the right hand: in the sinister, a female figure holding a ring. In the lower portion of the seal a Bishop is depicted kneeling. The inscription reads: REX.FURIT.   HEC.PLORAT. PATET.AURUM.   DUM.SACER.ORAT. This is almost certainly a pictorial representation of the legend of St. Mungo and the Queen of Cadzow's ring, and goes far to establish what may be called the " Kentigern theory " as to the derivation of the salmon and ring. The inscription may be translated, " The king is furious; she is weeping; while the saint prays, the golden ornament appears."

There has also survived a third seal of this Bishop, with a representation of the bird and salmon.

Then in mediæval times, the " tree," the bird, and the salmon were all used on the seals of the Bishops of the diocese, the prevailing device on the main part of the seal being, as might be expected, the patron saint himself; and the bell was used, together with the other three emblems, on the seal ad causas of the cathedral chapter, which was used from 1488-1540.

In pre-reformation times, then, the four emblems of St. Kentigern, the branch, the bird, the salmon, and the bell, are all found as devices on the seals of the Bishops and other ecclesiastical officials and communities. But it was not till after the Reformation that they came to be used in a heraldic manner: and the arrangement of the emblems as a heraldic charge was the work, not of the bishops of the diocese, but of the town authorities.

In the middle ages Glasgow was a Bishop's Burgh: the Provost was nominated by the Bishop, who also selected the Bailies from a list submitted to him by the Town Council. It was not till the eve of the reformation that Glasgow became an independent town.

We find, then, that the common seal of the town was derived from those of the Bishop and bore the four emblems arranged round the head of St. Kentigern, which occupied the centre of the round seal. This common seal was in use in 1325 and was still used as late as 1647. In that year (August 28th) a new seal appears bearing a variation of the arms now in use. This was not, however, the first appearance of the arms of Glasgow. In 1592 a shield was carved in the wall over the entrance of the Tron Church. This bore the device of a tree growing out of a salmon: a bird on the branches, and a bell hanging detached on the dexter side of the shield. The tree is eradicated, that is to say, the mount in the base of the shield is not yet there, and the bell is on the wrong, i.e. the dexter, side. This variation was placed on the old Grammar School in 1601; in Lauder's Chapter House in the Cathedral is a fragment bearing the same device; and it was also found on a stair in the inner quadrangle of the old College, which was not older than 1631.

On a bell made in Holland for the Tron steeple in 1631, is a shield of arms the design for which was sent from Glasgow to Holland, and on this shield the tree is shown for the first time growing from a mount in the base of the shield.

There are other examples of the arms of Glasgow used by the city authorities in the 17th century, but enough have been noticed to show the development of the shield.

We may now return to the ecclesiastical use of the arms. The earliest example is contained in a very interesting seal belonging to the Chapter of the Cathedral. The device on the seal is a church (? the Cathedral). In the open door is a tree growing, together with the salmon and bell: probably the redbreast was also there, but it cannot now be made out.

This seal was given to the Chapter by William Anderson, Provost of the city from 1664-1670. Thus while the four emblems of St. Kentigern were derived by the town from the diocese, it was the Provost of the town who gave them back to the diocese in the form of armorial bearings.

Two post-reformation Archbishops have left seals of heraldic interest :—

(1) Alexander Cairncross, 1684-1687, bore on his seal a shield, parted per pale : dexter, the assumed arms of the see: sinister, his paternal arms. In the diocesan arms there is no mount, the tree being " eradicated " and the bell is detached.

(2) John Paterson, Dean of Edinburgh, the last Archbishop of Glasgow, has left a round seal, which shows us another variation of the arms as usually borne : the seal bears a shield parted per pale : dexter, the arms very much as at present in use; but the arrangement of the emblems is reversed :

the bird and the salmon look to the sinister, and the bell hangs from the tree on the dexter side. There is also a chief charged with the demi-figure of St. Mungo : sinister, his paternal arms. The demi-figure of the Saint is not unlike the bust of St: Mungo at present used as the crest of the city.

(Andrew Fairfoul, 1661-1663, bore on his seal an ingenious device, viz., the Glasgow tree, among the branches of which was a shield bearing three fowls, his paternal arms, a kind of combination of official and personal arms.)

Both in mediæval and post-reformation times, then, we find devices used with reference to the traditional founder of the see and his miracles : and these devices in process of time developed into the present shield of arms.

As regards blazoning the arms, their origin should be kept in mind, and the tree should be blazoned as "*hazel*," instead of the "*oak*" recorded by the Town Council. And, though the bell in the arms of the city is blazoned in the Lyon Register, as "in the sinister fess point," i.e., not hanging from the tree, but detached, it would perhaps be more appropriate to attach the bell to the sinister side of the tree, in allusion to the practice of St. Mungo beside the Molendinar Burn, mentioned above. By so blazoning the arms of the diocese, we would avoid a slavish copy of the city armorial bearings, and as diocesan arms they would gain in significance from the allusion to the first Bishop.

The arms then may be blazoned thus :—

"*Argent, on a mount in base vert, a hazel tree ; pendent from a bough thereof on the sinister side an old quadrangular church bell; on the top of the tree a red-breast ; upon the stem at the base a salmon fessways on its back, holding in its mouth a signet ring, all proper.*"

CHAPTER XV.

Galloway.

The name of St. Ninian, the earliest known Scottish Bishop, must always be connected with the diocese of Galloway. He was the first Bishop of the ancient see : the cathedral was dedicated to him and St. Martin of Tours : his effigy is represented on the diocesan arms as recorded in the Lyon Register in the 17th century by Bishop John Paterson, son of the Bishop of Ross, who recorded the arms of that diocese.

The facts of the life of St. Ninian are very well known, but may be briefly set down. He was born at Witherne in Galloway in the fourth century; as a young man he went to Rome, where he spent several years, and was consecrated by the Bishop of Rome for the Western parts of Britain. On his way home he visited St. Martin at Tours, and from him he borrowed masons, who might build for him a church after the Roman manner. He chose Witherne in Galloway as the site of his church, and there he built what was reputed to be the first church constructed of stone in Britain. The building must have been in progress in the year 397, because, hearing of the death of St. Martin, which took place in that year, Ninian dedicated his church to him.

Bede's account (contained in Forbes' " Kalendars of Scottish Saints ") is of interest :—" The southern Picts who lived on this side of the mountains, had long before, as is reported, forsaken the error of idolatry, and embraced the truth by the preaching of Nynias, a most reverend Bishop and holy man of the British nation who had been regularly instructed at Rome in the faith and mysteries of the truth: whose episcopal see, named after St. Martin and the Bishop, and famous for a stately church (wherein he and many other saints rest in the body) is still existent among the English nation. The place belongs to the Bernicians, and is generally called Candida Casa, because he there built a church of stone, which was not usual among the Britons."

St. Ninian preached the gospel to great multitudes who came to be baptized, and it is recorded (by Aelred, a 12th century monk of Rievaulx, whose statements, however, are not always reliable) that he ordained Priests, consecrated Bishops, and divided the whole land "per certas parrochias." He died about the year 432.

The Bishops who ruled the diocese of Candida Casa, or Galloway, during the middle ages, have not left many seals: it should be remembered, by the way, that they were subject to the English Archbishop of York practically till the close of the middle ages. It was not until 1472 that the diocese became a part of the Scottish Church, when it was included in the province of St. Andrews by the Bull of Pope Sixtus IV. Twenty years later it was transferred to the province of Glasgow.

Those seals, however, that have come down to our time, bear as the main device an effigy of the first Bishop of the ancient see. One of them in particular presents a feature of special interest; Bishop Thomas Spens, 1449/50-1457 or 1458, bore on his seal the figure of a Bishop, clearly St. Ninian, holding a fetter in his right hand: on each side is a niche containing a fetter lock to secure both feet. Now the oldest seal of the Burgh of Whithorn has the representation of a sainted Bishop seated on what looks like a table or bench, and on each side of the Bishop are three links of a chain. The later burgh seal represented a saint with a chain and fetter lock hanging from his wrist. Laing takes this figure to be St. Leonard, no doubt on account of the chain, which was the recognised symbol of that saint, who was the patron of prisoners and slaves. But it seems incredible that the device of the chain and fetter lock used on both the burgh seals, and on that of at least one of the mediæval Bishops of the diocese, should refer to the foreign St. Leonard, who had no connection with the burgh or diocese, rather than with Ninian, who was a native of the place, and with whom the history both of the see and town was closely connected. The figure must be intended to represent the patron, and, as Lord Bute suggests, the fetters are no doubt allusive to the right of sanctuary possessed by the monastery and cathedral of Whithorn.

The seal of the chapter referred only indirectly to St. Ninian : it bore the representation of a building, which was probably intended to be the Candida Casa, the successor of the famous building of the founder of the see.

The seals of the post-reformation Bishops bore as a rule the paternal arms of their owners, but Bishop Paterson, who recorded the arms of the diocese at the Lyon Office, impaled those arms, which are at present in use, with his paternal arms. Thus both in the mediæval church and in the reformed, we find the figure of the patron saint used as the favourite device by the Bishops on their official seals.

In the shield of arms of the diocese, it would be appropriate and probably more correct, to blazon the links of chain, not only because they seem to have had a traditional connection with St. Ninian, but for the sake of their historical significance, as preserving the memory of one of the privileges enjoyed by the ancient cathedral of the diocese.

The arms are blazoned thus :—"*Argent, St. Ninian standing and full-faced proper, clothed with a pontifical robe proper, mitred and holding a crosier, or.*"

CHAPTER XVI.

Argyll.

The arms of the diocese of Argyll first appear, as far as we know, on the seal of Bishop Arthur Ross, who governed the see from 1675-1679. His seal, which was round in shape, bore a shield parted per pale: dexter, two crosiers endorsed saltirewise, in chief a mitre: sinister, the paternal arms of Ross. These diocesan arms he recorded in the Lyon Register.

There are two possible explanations of this shield of arms:

(1) The diocese of Argyll or Lismore was probably founded about the year 1200: it was not mentioned in the list of Scottish sees in the Bull of Pope Innocent III., who was crowned 1197-8. St. John Scot, Bishop of Dunkeld, whose jurisdiction extended to the extreme west of the country, is said to have asked the Pope to separate the western part of his diocese, as he, being an Englishman, did not understand the language of the people. The diocese of Argyll was therefore formed out of the parent see of Dunkeld, and Bishop John's Chaplain, Haraldus, became first Bishop about the year 1200. Walcot suggests that the second crosier in the shield of the arms of the diocese is allusive to the parent see of Dunkeld. (Scoti-Monasticon.)

(2) The arms may be derived from the famous crosier

of St. Moluag or Molocus, which is still in existence, in the possession of the Duke of Argyll. Moluag, according to the legend, was a Scot who was brought up by Brandan, a famous saint, celebrated, among other things, for being the father or Abbat of 3000 monks. St. Moluag early showed great piety, for when his fellow-disciples built houses for themselves, he built churches and altars for God. This saint was held in great honour during the middle ages, as the founder and first Bishop of the early see of Lismore, a little island in Loch Linnhe, where in later times the cathedral of the diocese of Argyll was built. There are strong grounds for supposing that another relic of this saint, in addition to his crosier, is still in existence, namely, his bell. According to Bishop Dowden (The Celtic Church in Scotland), the Kilmichael Glassary Bell with its twelfth century shrine, now in the National Museum of Antiquities in Edinburgh, is probably none other than the bell of St. Moluag which was famed throughout the middle ages. St. Moluag is said to have retired from Lismore to Ross, where he became associated with St. Boniface, and was buried in the cathedral of Rosemarkie.

St. Moluag then, being reverenced in the mediæval diocese as the reputed founder of the ancient see, and as the patron of the cathedral church at Lismore, it is not surprising to find that a representation of a sainted Bishop (i.e., with a halo) is the prevailing device on the seals of the mediæval Bishops : and it is not difficult to identify the figure with the patron.

The early Bishops of every see in Scotland bore on their seals the device of a Bishop in the act of benediction, but as time went on, some device, allusive as a rule to the dedication of the cathedral or to the patron of the diocese, became the general custom. But in the diocese of Argyll, as in the dioceses of Glasgow and Galloway, the patrons of the cathedrals and sees were bishops; so an Episcopal figure remains the prevailing device in these sees throughout the middle ages, while generally the owner of the seal is represented in an attitude of adoration in the base of the seal. In the case of Argyll the sainted Bishop, whom we may assume to be St. Moluag, appears on the seal or on one of the seals of every mediæval Bishop whose seals have come down to us. The first is that of Bishop Alan; there is represented St. Moluag; and in the base, the Bishop adoring his patron. Later Bishops also bore their paternal arms.

From an examination of the seals of the mediæval Bishops, then, the weight of such evidence as there is, is rather in favour of the second interpretation of the shield of arms, namely, that the crosiers are borne in allusion to the famous old crosier of the saint who, according to tradition, had so close a connection with the diocese. But the evidence, it must be admitted, is so meagre, that it is much more probable, when we remember that in 1675 the palmy days of the science of heraldry were past, that the arms assumed for the see are merely of a conventional nature. However this may be, the choice of crosiers as the heraldic bearings of the diocese was in this case a happy coincidence.

The arms are blazoned thus:—"*Azure, two crosiers in saltire and in chief a mitre, or.*"

CHAPTER XVII.

The Isles.

In the nineteenth century the Lyon King of Arms granted armorial bearings to the newly-founded college of Cumbrae. And this shield bore as its first and fourth quarterings the arms which had been previously assumed for the diocese of the Isles. The shield of the see represents St. Columba, the patron of the diocese and of the Monastery at Iona, in a coracle holding in his left hand a dove, and looking towards a blazing star. The story of St. Columba, his mission to the Picts, and his foundation of the monastery at Iona, are so well known that there is no need to relate them here: suffice it to say that we shall find reference to the saint and his work in the seals of mediæval Bishops of Sodor or The Isles, and more especially in those of the post-reformation Bishops.

Of the seals of the pre-reformation Bishops, only very few have survived, two of them of early date. On these two seals, which belonged to Bishop Richard (consecrated in 1252-3 by the Archbishop of Trondhjem, to which metropolitan the see of the Isles was then subject), and Bishop Mark, his successor, there appears the device of a Bishop. This figure may possibly have been intended to represent the Abbat Columba. John Campbell, provided to the bishopric in 1486-7, bore on his seal a figure of St. Columba, which can be identified beyond doubt by the nimbus and by the dove which he is holding : in the base of the seal is a shield bearing the Bishop's paternal arms.

There is one interesting indication of the existence of a diocesan badge or emblem. On the famous heraldic ceiling of the cathedral of Aberdeen there are depicted the paternal arms of the Bishops who occupied the Scottish sees in 1520. In that year the diocese of The Isles was vacant; and instead of leaving the shield which was intended to bear the arms of the B:shop of that see blank, or omitting it altogether, there was carved on it as a charge a dove displayed, a play on the name Columba. Though this cannot, of course, be regarded as a diocesan shield of arms, it may be recognised as an example of the use of a symbol of St. Columba as the badge of the see during a vacancy.

Three post-reformation Bishops have left seals showing different versions of the device borne on the arms of the diocese at the present time : so we have, with the modern arms three variations :—

(1) The seal of Bishop Andrew Knox, 1605. On it is shown St. Columba in an open boat, holding in his left hand a book. This is no doubt an allusion to the book of the Gospels, the translating of which, according to tradition, was the cause of his exile from his home in Ireland.

(2) The seals of Bishop Nigel Campbell, 1634, and Bishop Robert Wallace, 1661, show a figure of St. Columba in a boat, rowed by three men: this probably is a representation of the following incident :—" On one occasion, while St. Columba was at sea, a tempest came on, and the waves dashed over the ship. He was helping the sailors to bale out the water. 'What you do now,' they cried, 'can be of little use. Pray for us rather, else we perish.' He ceased from his work, and standing on the prow, stretched out his hands to

heaven, and prayed fervently. That same hour the storm abated." (Grub.)

(3) The arms at present in use. They are probably a representation of the same incident as that depicted in (2), though the sailors have been omitted. But Baring Gould connects the shield with the see of Man, and identifies the saint with St. Mauchold, and the legend that he committed himself to the waves to find a sphere of mission work under the guidance of God.

But in spite of variations, the main design of the three devices is practically the same, St. Columba in an open boat; for the history of the development of the arms points to the correctness of the Columba-interpretation as against the theory of Baring Gould. I think that there can be no doubt that the arms, as at present used, are a representation of an incident in the life of the patron of the see.

They are blazoned in the Lyon Register as the first and fourth quarters of the arms of the College of the Holy Spirit, Cumbrae, thus :—"*Azure, St. Columba in a boat at sea, in his sinister hand a dove, and in the dexter chief a blazing star, all proper.*"

CHAPTER XVIII.

Marshalling.

Marshalling is the arrangement of different Coats of Arms on one shield. Arms may be thus grouped to indicate marriage, office, or the union of territories, nations, or dioceses.

In cases of personal arms there are many possible combinations and in consequence many rules to be observed, but we have only to deal with :—

(1) Diocesan arms combined with the paternal arms of the Bishop.

(2) Arms of dioceses which have been united to meet the needs of the Church.

Official arms are impaled with the paternal arms of the holder of the office. (When arms are impaled, the shield is divided into two equal parts perpendicularly, and the two coats are placed in their entirety, one in either half.) The official arms as the more honourable occupy the dexter side. In the middle ages official arms were practically unknown in Scotland, and Diocesan arms were not used until after the Reformation, when the custom was borrowed from England. It then became the custom of the Scottish Bishops to impale their family arms with those of their sees, as did the English Bishops. It is true that the custom of impaling paternal with official arms has never become general in Scotland, but in view of the fact that the custom of impaling the arms of the Bishop with those of the see is as old as the practice of bearing diocesan arms, there is much to be said for the continuance of the custom.

As regards the grouping of diocesan arms, it must be remembered that these are not personal, but fall into the category of Arms of Dominion, or of Inferior Dominion. Different methods have been employed:—

(1) *Impalement*: the meaning of this term has already been explained. It is usually associated with marriage, when the husband impales the arms of his wife with his own, or with arms of office, but there are also a few cases on record where the impaled arms indicate unions of fiefs or dominions. Stevenson (Heraldry in Scotland) cites the case of Lord Ruthven and Dirleton who in 1550 and 1560 inherited the honours of both his father and his mother, and afterwards used a seal with his father's and mother's arms *per pale*. This may possibly be an example of impaled arms alluding to the union of two fiefs as by marriage.

There is also the case of the Royal arms used by Queen Anne, in the first and fourth quarters of which are displayed the arms of France and England *parted per pale*.

This is the customary manner in which are combined the arms of the united dioceses of Aberdeen and Orkney, Glasgow and Galloway, and Argyll and The Isles. It was by impalement, too, that the arms of the Dioceses of Gloucester and Bristol were combined during the union of those sees in the 19th century. But in view of the scanty precedents it is doubtful whether this is the best method to be adopted.

(2) The more usual method of grouping Arms of Dominion was *quartering*, that is, dividing the shield into four parts *per cross*, or into a larger number of " quarters," for the term " Quarter " in heraldry is not confined to the fourth part of the whole.

The ancient arms of the English Kings were, *quarterly*,

France and England, indicating the royal claim to dominion over the two countries.

The modern Royal Arms of Great Britain and Ireland, though they are the personal arms of the Sovereign, inasmuch as no subject may lawfully display them or make use of them, are in reality Arms of Dominion, which are borne by the King in virtue of his office in place of the Arms of Saxe Coburg Gotha, which are his family arms in accordance with the laws of heraldry.

Now here we have two examples of Arms of Dominion, the one indicating the (theoretical) union of two kingdoms, and the other the union of three. In both cases the combined arms are borne quarterly.

This method has distinct advantage over the present haphazard methods of grouping the arms of united dioceses, not only as being more in accordance with precedent, but also as affording a system by which the arms of two or of three dioceses can be grouped in a uniform manner.

At the present time there are in Scotland three groups of two, and two groups of three, united dioceses. The former consist of Aberdeen and Orkney, Glasgow and Galloway, and Argyll and The Isles, the latter of St. Andrews, Dunkeld and Dunblane, and Moray, Ross and Caithness. The manner in which the arms of the former groups are marshalled has been on the whole uniform, namely, by impalement, but there has been much diversity of use in the case of the latter. The correct method of arranging the arms of both the united dioceses is that commonly followed in the Diocese of St. Andrews, Dunkeld, and Dunblane, where the arms of St. Andrews occupy the first and fourth quarters, Dunkeld the second, and Dunblane the third. (Strictly speaking, on the analogy of the Royal arms, in the Diocese of Dunkeld the arms of that see should be placed in the first and fourth quarters, and the arms of

Dunblane should be similarly arranged, when the arms are used in connection with that diocese.)

But there are variations in use: for instance, St. Andrews is sometimes made to occupy the whole of the dexter half of the shield, while the sinister side is divided horizontally between Dunkeld and Dunblane. If this arrangement means anything, it means that St. Andrews once married Dunkeld, who unfortunately died, and St. Andrews consoled himself with Dunblane. Another rather unsatisfactory arrangement of the arms of this united diocese is that used on the Bishop Wilkinson memorial in St. Ninian's Cathedral at Perth. There the shield is divided *per pale and chevron;* i.e., a perpendicular line is dropped from the middle of the top to the central point of the shield: from this point two lines are drawn to the lower parts of the sides of the shield in the form of a chevron, dividing the shield into three more or less equal compartments. In these are displayed the coats of arms of the three dioceses. This is a method almost unknown to British Heraldry, though it is not uncommon on the Continent. It occurs, for instance, in German Heraldry in the arms of Hanover, where the shield is "*tierced in pairle reversed,*" the three compartments being occupied by the arms of Brunswick, Luneburg, and Westphalia.

The arrangement at present in use of the arms of the Diocese of Moray, Ross, and Caithness is even more unsatisfactory. The shield is divided *per pale,* dexter the arms of Moray, sinister those of Ross, while the coat of Caithness occupies the whole base of the shield, an arrangement which appears to be based on no law of heraldry.

If, then, the arms of the united dioceses are to be grouped on shields, the most satisfactory and probably the most correct course would be to adopt the uniform method of quartering.

There is, however, one fact which should not be left out of account. In the case of families and states where different coats of arms have been quartered on the same shield, it has been done in view of the fact that the union, which the coat of arms was to indicate, was intended to be a lasting one. Now in the case of the Church, this intention does not exist: the combination of dioceses which exists at present is not permanent; the arrangement of the dioceses has been altered from time to time in the past, and no doubt will undergo more changes in the future to meet the varying needs of the Church; in fact, the whole system of united dioceses is a temporary expedient born of the present numerical weakness of the Church. Keeping this fact in view, it might be well to adopt what was perhaps the oldest method of marshalling arms, that is by placing the two or the three shields side by side, and not grouping them on one shield. Shields so arranged are said to be *accolee*. This system would emphasize the fact that each of the ancient dioceses is still a separate entity, though perhaps combined with others as a temporary expedient, framed to meet the Church's present needs. The Bishop's paternal arms would then be impaled with each of his diocesan coats.

NOTE.—It should be borne in mind that from the legal point of view there is no question of marshalling the arms of the Scottish Bishoprics. In no united diocese of the Episcopal Church are both or all three coats registered at the Lyon office, and, whether the Church has a right to bear the registered coats or not, the use of those which have never been matriculated is certainly illegal.

CHAPTER XIX.

The Legal Question.

In discussing the legal right of the Episcopal Church to bear Arms, there are two distinct questions to be answered :—

(1) The question of general principle. Is a diocese in a Presbyterian country so far recognized as to be able to claim the privilege of bearing arms?

(2) Is the disestablished Church in Scotland entitled to continue the use of the five particular coats of arms which were recorded at the Lyon office during the period of its legal establishment?

In the first question is involved the further question, to whom do we assume these arms to belong? are they the official arms of the Bishop himself, or are they the arms of the diocese as a corporate body?

Official arms are few and far between in Scottish Heraldry : the Lyon King of Arms was granted arms in virtue of his office : so was the Master of the Revels in Scotland; but with one or two exceptions the use of official arms was almost unknown in this country. It has already been shown that during the middle ages Bishops as a general custom used their paternal arms with external additions indicative of their office, such as Mitre and Crozier : and such is still the general rule in Scottish Heraldry with respect to the arms of those who hold high office.

But, on the other hand, the mediæval Bishops occasionally bore on their seals arms indicating the territory in which their diocese lay : in other words, such arms had reference rather to the Bishop's sphere of jurisdiction than to his Episcopal office. And it was on these lines that the Episcopal Heraldry of Scotland developed. The armorial bearings of many dioceses are identical with those of the city from which the diocese derives its name, or where its cathedral was situated. The arms of St. Andrews, Aberdeen, Moray, Ross, Brechin, Glasgow, Galloway, are all in a greater or less degree derived from those of their cathedral cities. This would seem to indicate that the arms were intended to be diocesan rather than merely the official insignia of the Bishop.

If this is the case, there is not much further difficulty. Corporate bodies, it is generally conceded, have the right to record and bear arms, or to receive a grant of arms from the Lyon King. The Lyon Register contains records of the arms of burghs, universities, banks, merchant companies, schools, etc., and among the records of arms granted to colleges are those of the College of the Holy Spirit at Cumbrae. Now these arms granted by the Lyon King in recent times have a double significance : not only was it a grant of arms made to a college which has no connection with the State, but as has already been noted (chap. xvii), the first and fourth quarters consist of the armorial insignia borne of custom by the diocese of·the Isles. This seems to be a recognition on the part of the highest heraldic authority in Scotland of the general principle that a disestablished Church has a right to bear arms, and that a diocese as such is under no disability in this respect.

But while there is little doubt that there are at least reasonable grounds for assuming that a diocese has a right to arms, yet it must be remembered that under the law of 1672 the assumption of arms, except under the authority of the Lyon Court, is forbidden under severe penalties. Of the fourteen dioceses in Scotland, the arms of only five—St. Andrews, Edinburgh, Ross, Galloway and Argyll—have been registered in accordance with the law, all of them previous to the disestablishment of the Church.

The interesting question now arises : is the disestablished Church entitled to continue the use of those particular coats of arms which belonged to it during its legal connection with the State? or did the armorial bearings share the fate of the dioceses when they were legally abolished? or are they the legal property of the present establishment, together with the endowments and other property of the old undivided Church of Scotland?

The chief difficulty is the lack of precedent. The case of the Church of Ireland affords the nearest parallel, and there the practice of bearing diocesan arms has continued in spite of the disestablishment. Of course the two Churches are not in quite the same position; in Ireland no other Communion was set up by law in the place of the old national Church, and therefore no claim can be put forward by any other body.

In Scotland the problem is not so easy of solution, being complicated by the existence of the Established Church, which succeeded to the rights, privileges and property of the ancient Church. But it must not be forgotten that diocesan arms came into existence during the periods of the reformed Episcopacy; they were not among the possessions of the mediæval Scottish Church, but in their origin they belong purely to the " Episcopal " Church. In any case the present Established Church has laid no claim to their possession, so in all probability any claim which it might have had has lapsed during the past two centuries.

A recent writer on Scottish Heraldry, referring to this question, says : " Who, if anyone, since the Revolution Settlement have right to those arms has, so far as we know, never been decided" (Stevenson, "Heraldry in Scotland," 1914). In the year following the publication of this work, a case was tried in the Lyon Court which, though not an exact analogy, has curious points of resemblance to the problem which is under our consideration.

The history of the case was this :—In 1914 Roderick Ambrose Macneil, Chief of the Macneils of Barra, died in the United States of America, being still a British citizen, leaving two sons. Paul Humphrey Macneil, the elder son, in his father's life time renounced his allegiance to the British Crown and became an American citizen; in consequence of this his father in 1913 nominated his second son, Robert Lister Macneil, the petitioner, to succeed him as Chief of the Clan, and assigned to him the arms pertaining to the Chief. Robert Lister Macneil therefore petitioned the Lyon King to grant him the arms recorded by General Roderick Macneil in 1824, which were borne by his (the petitioner's father), Roderick Ambrose Macneil.

In the course of his decision the Lyon King of Arms said :—

> "In the present case the Petitioner asks to be allowed to record the arms registered in 1824 by the undoubted head of his family, General Roderick Macneil. If these were allowed him, it follows that his elder brother and the senior line in future generations would be deprived of arms altogether, i.e., of the arms to which they would otherwise be entitled. The elder brother is an American citizen and cannot therefore take out a new grant of arms for himself : but he has a perfect right, if he chooses, to matriculate in his own name the arms recorded by his kinsman in 1824, as the right to matriculate arms is one which depends on descent alone and has nothing to do with nationality.

● ● ● ● ● ●

"It appears to be the general opinion of writers on the subject that a chief has the power of such nomination, though in all probability it was homologated by the clan in general, or the leading members of it, acting for the community at large."

He accordingly granted the Petitioner, i.e., the younger son, the arms recorded by General Roderick Macneil in 1824, together with supporters (Highland Chiefs being entitled to such honourable additaments), *but the arms were to be differenced as for a second son.*

The force of this decision was that while the younger son was granted the chiefship with all such privileges as attach to it on the nomination of his father, the late Chief, and in the absence of opposition from the clan, the right of the elder brother to the undiminished paternal arms was not prejudiced, even though he had become an American citizen.

This decision has a strong bearing on the position of the Scottish Episcopal Church. There are several points of resemblance between the position of the elder Macneil and that of the disestablished Church :—

(1) The elder brother severs his connection with the British State : the Episcopal Church by disestablishment lost its State relationship.

(2) The younger son gets the title of Chief with such honours and privileges as pertain to it : the Presbyterian Church became the "Established" Church of Scotland with the privileges and endowments belonging to the position.

(3) The choice of the younger son by his father was homologated by the clan : the establishment of the Presbyterian Church was and is approved by the majority of the nation.

(4) But the family arms still belong to the alien

elder brother and his heirs after him *jure sanguinis* there are therefore strong grounds for assuming that the dioceses of the Episcopal Church in Scotland, which, though no longer legally connected with the State, still exist " in dutiful allegiance to the King," enjoy unimpaired their right to their ancient arms.

To sum up briefly :—

1. The principle that dioceses as corporate bodies may bear arms, even when the Church itself is disestablished, appears to have been recognised by the Lyon Court in the grant of arms made to the College of the Holy Spirit, Cumbrae.

2. The claim of the dioceses to bear those particular arms which were recorded by them before disestablishment is supported by the practice of the Church of Ireland; by the fact that the Presbyterian Church has laid no claim to them, the practice of bearing arms having arisen in post-reformation Episcopal times; and by the decision of the Lord Lyon King of Arms in the petition of the Macneil of Barra.

INDEX.

Aberdeen: Arms of City, 33, 36; Cathedral Heraldic ceiling, 10, 34, 76; Chapter Seal, 35; King's College, 35.
Aberdeen: Arms of Diocese, 9, 33-36, 86.
Aberdeen and Orkney, Arms of, 80.
Abernethy, 23, 25; Arms of, 26.
Accolée, 83.
Achievement, 5.
Alan, Bishop of Argyll, 73.
Anderson, William, Provost of Glasgow, 64.
Andrew, St., 16; Colours of, 7.
Anne, Queen, Royal Arms of, 80.
Annulet, 51.
Argyll: Arms of Diocese, 8, 9, 13, 71-73; Foundation of Diocese, 71.
Argyll and the Isles, Arms of, 80.

Beaton, James, Archbishop of Glasgow and St. Andrews, 19.
Bend, 7.
"Bishop of the Scots," 18, 19.
Blane, St., 27, 28.
Boke of St. Albans, 2.
Boniface, St., 45-46, 72.
Bothwell, Adam, Bishop of Orkney, 39.
Brandan, St., 72.
Brechin: Arms of City, 53, 54, 55; Seal of City, 54; Cathedral Dedication, 53, 56.
Brechin: Arms of Diocese, 9, 12, 13, 53-56, 86.
Brechin, Henry, Lord of, 53.

Cairncross, Alexander, Archbishop of Glasgow, 64.
Caithness: Arms of Diocese, 9, 49-52.

Caithness: Arms of Earldom, 50, 51.
Campbell, John, Bishop of the Isles, 75.
Campbell, Nigel, Bishop of the Isles, 76.
Candida Casa, 68.
Cathures (Glasgow), 60.
Celtic Church, 11.
Charges, 8, 9.
Charles I, King, 31, 32.
Chevron, 7.
Chief, 7.
Colours, 6.
Columba, St., 35, 75, 76, 77.
Coventre, Walter de, Bishop of Dunblane, 27.
Crest, 10.
Crichton, George, Bishop of Dunkeld, 24.
Cross, 7.
Crusades, 3.
Cumbrae College: Grant of Arms, 75, 77, 86.
Cuthbert, St., 32.

David, St.: 60.
Diocesan Arms, Adoption of, 13.
Dornoch Cathedral, 49.
Douglas, Gavin, Bishop of Dunkeld, 24, 25.
Douglas, Robert, Bishop of Dunblane, 27, 29.
Drummond, James, Bishop of Brechin, 54.
Duffield, Nicholas, Bishop of Dunkeld, 24.
Dunbar, Gavin, Bishop of Aberdeen, 35.
Dunblane: Arms of Diocese, 9, 14, 27-29; Chapter Seal, 28.
Dundee: Arms on Church Tower, 55.

Dunkeld: Arms of Diocese, 9, 23-26; Chapter Seal, 25.

Edinburgh: Arms of City, 41; St. Giles', 31; Chapter Seal, 43.
Edinburgh: Arms of Diocese, 9, 12, 13, 31-32.
Elgin: Burgh Seal, 41; Cathedral, 42; Chapter Seal, 42—43.
England, Ancient Arms of, 80.

Fairfoul, Andrew, Archbishop of Glasgow, 65.
Fess, 7.
Fortrose Cathedral, 46; Chapter Seal, 47.
Fraser, John, Bishop of Ross, 47.
Fraser, William, Bishop of St. Andrews, 18.
Fulzie, Archdeacon of Orkney, 39.
Furs, 6.

Galley or Lymphad, 50, 52.
Galloway: Arms of Diocese, 6 note, 9, 13, 67-69, 86.
Gilbert, St., Bishop of Caithness, 49-50.
Giles, St., 32, 41-42.
Gladstanes, George, Archbishop of St. Andrews, 20.
Glasgow: Arms of City, 57, 63, 64; Burgh Seal, 63; Cathedral, 61, 63; Chapter Seal, 63, 64.
Glasgow: Arms of Diocese, 9, 13, 14, 57-65, 86.
Glasgow and Galloway, Arms of, 8, 80.
Graham, Patrick, Archbishop of St. Andrews, 18.
Guthrie, John, Bishop of Moray, 42.

Haliburton, George, Bishop of Brechin, 54.

Hamilton, John, Bishop of Dunkeld, 24.
Hanover, Arms of, 82.
Haraldus, Bishop of Argyll, 71.
Harold, King of Norway, 37.
Hat, Ecclesiastical, 9.
Helmet, 9.
Honeyman, Andrew, Bishop of Orkney, 29.
Hunter, Abbat, of Melrose, 11.
Huntingdon, David, Earl of, 53.

Impalement, 79.
Innocent III., Pope, 71.
Iona, Monastery at, 75.
Ireland, Church of, 87.
Isles: Arms of Diocese, 13, 75-77.
Isles, Lord of the, Arms, 50.
Israel, Tribal Ensigns of, 3.

John, St., the Scot, 71.

Kennedy, John, Bishop of St. Andrews, 18.
Kenneth Macalpin, King of Scots and Picts, 23.
Kentigern, St., 58, 59-61, 62.
Kilmichael Glassary Bell, 72.
Kilrymont, 17.
Kirkwall Cathedral, 37, 38; Chapter Seal, 29.
Knox, Andrew, Bishop of the Isles, 76.

Lambrequin or Mantling, 9.
Landallis, William de, Bishop of St. Andrews, 18, 19.
Lauder, Bishop of Dunkeld, 26.
Lawrence, St., 28.
Lawrence, St., of Canterbury, 28.
Leighton, Robert, Bishop of Dunblane, 9, 28.
Leonard, St., 69.
Lindsay, Alexander, Bishop of Dunkeld, 25.

Lindsay, David, Bishop of Edinburgh, 31.
Lindsay, John de, Bishop of Glasgow, 62.
Lismore, 71; Cathedral, 72.
Locrys (Leuchars), Patrick, Bishop of Brechin, 53.
Lyon King of Arms, 13, 75, 85.

Machar, St., 35.
Macneil, General Roderick, 88.
Macneil, Robert Lister, 88.
Macneil, Roderick Ambrose of Barra, 88.
Magnus Barefoot, King of Norway, 37.
Magnus, St., 37, 38.
Mains, Arms in Church at, 55.
Malcolm Ceanmore, 17.
Margaret, St., 17.
Mark, Bishop of the Isles, 75.
Marshalling, 79.
Martin, St., 67.
Mauchold, St., 77.
Maxwell, Bishop of Orkney, 39.
Maxwell, John, Bishop of Ross, 47.
Meldrum, Thomas, 54.
Metals, 6.
Mitre, 9.
Moluag, St., 72.
Moray: Arms of Diocese, 9, 41-43, 86.
Moray: Arms of Province, 42.
Moray, Ross, and Caithness, Arms of, 12, 81, 82.
Mungo, St., see Kentigern.
Murray, Thomas, Bishop of Caithness, 50.

Nectan, King of Pictavia, 46.
Nicholas, St., 33, 34.
Nidrie, Thomas, Archdeacon of Moray, 9.
Ninian, St., 54, 60, 67, 68, 69.
Nisbet of Dean, 13,

Official Arms, 79, 85
Ordinaries, 7-9.

Orkney: Arms of Diocese, 9, 37-40.

Pale, 7.
Paterson, John, Archbishop of Glasgow, 64.
Paterson, John, Bishop of Ross, 45.
Paterson, Bishop of Galloway, 69.
Peter, St., 46, 47, 48; Colours, 48.
Pile, 56.
Pilmore, John, Bishop of Moray, 42.
" Pontificals," 36.
Prebenda, Robert de, Bishop of Dunblane, 27

Quartering, 80.

Ramsay, James, Bishop of Dunblane, 27.
Ramsay, James, Bishop of Ross, 48.
Register of the Lord Lyon, 13, 20, 31, 33, 45, 65, 67, 71, 77, 86.
Regulus, St., 16.
Richard, Bishop of the Isles, 75.
Robert I., Bishop of Ross, 47.
Robert II., Bishop of Ross, 47, 48.
Robert, Bishop of St. Andrews, 18.
Roger, Bishop of Ross, 47.
Rose, Bishop of Edinburgh, 31.
Rosemarkie Cathedral, 45, 72.
Ross: Arms of Diocese, 9, 13, 45-48.
Ross: Arms of Province, 47.
Ross, Arthur, Bishop of Argyll, 71.
Royal Arms, 25, 80-81.
Ruthven and Dirleton, Seal of Lord, 80.

St. Andrews: Arms of Diocese, 9, 13, 15-21, 86.

St. Andrews, Dunkeld, and Dunblane, Arms of, 8, 81-82.
Saltire, 7.
"Santa Claus," 35.
Seals, Episcopal, 12.
Serf, St., 59, 60.
Sharp, James, Archbishop of St. Andrews, 9, 20.
Shield, 5.
Sixtus IV., Pope, 17, 68.
Sodor, see Isles.
Spens, Thomas, Bishop of Galloway, 68.
Steward, Alexander, Bishop of Ross, 47.
Strachan, David, Bishop of Brechin, 54.
Stuart, Andrew, Bishop of Caithness, 51.
Subordinate Ordinaries, 7.
Supporters, 10, 89

Thenew, St. 59.
Tinctures, 5, 6.
Torse, see Wreath.
Tournament, 3.
Tressure, 7, 8, 19, 50.

Trinity, Representation on Seals, 42, 54, 56.
Tuathal, Bishop of Fortrenn, " Primus Episcopus," 23.
Tulloch, Bishop de, of Orkney, 39.
Turgot, Bishop of St. Andrews, 17.

Ungus, King of Picts, 17.

Virgin Mary; Colours, 7.

Wallace, Robert, Bishop of the Isles, 76.
Whithorn Burgh Seal, 68; Cathedral, 69; Chapter Seal, 69.
William, Bishop of Caithness, 49.
William, Bishop of Dunblane, 27.
Wischard, Robert, Bishop of Glasgow, 62.
Wishart, George, Bishop of Edinburgh, 31.
Wreath, 10.

www.armorial-register.com

www.ingramcontent.com/pod-product-compliance
Lightning Source LLC
Chambersburg PA
CBHW061446040426
42450CB00007B/1237